Bible Studies for Children

Matthew

© 2011 Nazarene Publishing House
ISBN 978-1-63580-084-5

Editor for US English version: Kimberly D. Adams
Director of Children's Ministries International: Leslie M. Hart
Managing Editor for Global English: Allison L. G. Southerland
Executive Editor for non-English versions: Allison L. G. Southerland
Editorial Committee: Dan Harris, Nate Owens, Beula Postlewait
Cover Art: Greg White

Published by
Kidz First Publications
17001 Prairie Star Parkway
Lenexa, KS 66220 (USA)
in cooperation with Children's Ministries International

This edition published by arrangement
with Nazarene Publishing House
Kansas City, Missouri USA

The first Children's Bible Quiz, created by Rev. William (Bill) Young, was
introduced with three demonstration teams from the Kansas City District
– Kansas City First, Kansas City St. Pauls, and Overland Park – at the 1968
General Nazarene Young People's Society Convention in Kansas City, Missouri (USA).

contents

welcome

WELCOME!

Welcome to *Bible Studies for Children: Matthew!* In this collection of biblical studies, the children learn about God's holiness and his faithfulness to his people, even when they make bad choices.

Bible Studies for Children: Matthew is one of six books in the *Bible Studies for Children* series. These studies help children to gain an understanding of biblical chronology and the meaning of biblical events. As the children learn about the lives of the people in these studies, they discover God's love for all people and their place in his plan. God sometimes uses miracles to achieve his purpose. He often works through people to accomplish what he wants to do.

The philosophy of *Bible Studies for Children* is to help the children to understand what the Bible says, to learn how God helped the people, and to know God through a relationship with him. This includes biblical study, biblical memorization, and application of biblical teachings in real life situations.

Bible Studies for Children uses the *New International Version* of the Bible.

BOOKS

The following is a short description of the books in this series and the way that they interact with each other.

Genesis provides the foundation. This book tells how God created the world from nothing, formed a man and a woman, and created a beautiful garden for their home. These people sinned, and they experienced the consequences for their sin. Genesis introduces the plan of God to reconcile the broken relationship between God and the people. It introduces Adam, Eve, Noah, Abraham, Isaac, and Jacob. God made a covenant with Abraham (in Genesis 15) and renewed that covenant with Isaac and Jacob. Genesis ends with the story of Joseph who saves civilization from famine. The famine compels the people of God to move to Egypt.

Exodus tells how God continued to keep his promise to Abraham in Genesis 15. God rescued the Israelites from the slavery in Egypt. The Lord chose Moses to guide the Israelites. The Lord set up his kingship over the Israelites. He led and ruled the Israelites through the establishment of the priesthood and the Tabernacle, the Ten Commandments and other laws, and the prophets and the judges. At the end of Exodus, only a part of the covenant of the Lord with Abraham is complete.

Joshua/Judges/Ruth tells how God completed his covenant that began in Genesis 15. Finally, the Israelites conquered and settled into the land that God promised to Abraham. The prophets, the priests, the Law, and the worship rituals declared that God was the Lord and the King of the Israelites. The 12 tribes of Israel settled into the promised land. This study emphasizes these judges: Deborah, Gideon, and Samson.

In **1 and 2 Samuel,** the Israelites wanted a king because the other nations had a king. These books tell about Samuel, Saul, and David. Jerusalem became the center of the combined nation of Israel. This study shows how the people react differently when someone confronted them with their sins. While Saul blamed others or used an excuse, David admitted his sin, and he asked God for forgiveness.

Matthew is the focal point of the entire series. It focuses on the birth, the life, and the ministry of Jesus. All the previous books in the series pointed to Jesus as the Son of God and the Messiah. Jesus ushered in a new era. The children learn about this new era in several events: the teachings of Jesus, his death, his resurrection, and the mentoring of his disciples. Through Jesus, God provided a new way for the people to have a relationship with him.

At the beginning of **Acts,** Jesus ascended to heaven, and God sent the Holy Spirit to help the Church. The good news of salvation through Jesus Christ spread to many parts of the world. The believers preached the gospel to the Gentiles, and missionary work began. The message of the love of God transformed both the Jews and the Gentiles. There is a direct connection between the evangelism efforts of Paul and Peter to the lives of the people today.

CYCLE

The following study cycle is suggested specifically for those who will participate in the optional Quizzing aspect of *Bible Studies for Children.*
Matthew (2011-12)
*Acts (2012-13)
Genesis (2013-14)
Exodus (2014-15)
Joshua/Judges/Ruth (2015-16)
*1 & 2 Samuel (2016-17)
Matthew (2017-2018)

* Indicates a World Quiz year.

SCHEDULE

Bible Studies for Children has twenty studies. Allow 60 to 120 minutes of class time. The following schedule is a suggestion for each study.

· 15 minutes for Activity
· 30 minutes for Biblical Lesson
· 15 minutes for Memory Verse
· 30 minutes for Additional Activities (optional)
· 30 minutes for Quizzing Practice (optional)

PREPARE

Thorough preparation of each study is important. The children are more attentive and gain better understanding of the study if the teacher prepares it well and presents it well. **Bold** text in each study indicates suggested words for the teacher to say to the children. The following steps are some guidelines for the teacher as he or she prepares each study.

Step 1: Quick Overview. Read the Memory Verse, Biblical Truth, Focus, and Teaching Tip.

Step 2: Bible Passage and Biblical Commentary. Read the verses in the Bible study passage and the information in the Biblical Commentary, and any Words of Our Faith, People, Places, or Things.

Step 3: Activity. This section includes a game or other activity to prepare the children for the biblical lesson. Become familiar with the activity, the instructions, and the supplies. Bring any necessary supplies to the class with you. Set up the activity before the children arrive.

Step 4: Biblical Lesson. Review the lesson and learn it so that you tell it as a story. The children want the teacher to tell the story rather than to read it from the book. Use the Words of Our Faith, People, Places, and Things from each lesson to provide additional information as you tell the story. After the story, use the review questions. They will help the children to understand the story and to apply it to their lives.

Step 5: Memory Verse. Learn the memory verse before you teach it to the children. A list of the memory verses and suggested memory verse activities are on pages 135-138. Choose from the activities to help the children to learn the memory verse. Become familiar with the activity that you choose. Read the instructions and prepare the supplies. Bring with you to the class any necessary supplies.

Step 6: Additional Activities. The additional activities are an optional part of the study. These activities will enhance the children's biblical study. Many of these activities require additional supplies, resources, and time. Become familiar with the activities that you choose. Read the instructions and prepare the supplies. Bring with you to the class any necessary supplies.

Step 7: Quizzing Practice. Quizzing is the competition part of *Bible Studies for Children.* Quizzing is an optional part of the study. If you choose to participate in Quizzing, spend time with the children in their preparation. There are practice questions for each study. The first ten questions are for a basic level of competition. There are three possible answers for each question, and these questions are simpler. The next ten questions are for an advanced level of the competition. There are four possible answers for each question, and these questions are more comprehensive. Children, with the guidance from their teacher, choose their level for the competition. Based on the number of children and the resources that are available, you may choose to offer only the Basic Level or only the Advanced Level. Before you ask the practice questions, read the scripture passage to the children.

children's Bible quizzing

CHILDREN'S BIBLE QUIZZING

Children's Bible Quizzing is an optional part of *Bible Studies for Children*. Each church and each child decides whether to participate in a series of competitive events.

Quizzing events follow the rules outlined in this book. Children do not compete against each other to determine a single winner. Churches do not compete against each other to determine a winner.

The purpose of Quizzing is to help the children to determine what they learned about the Bible, to enjoy the competitive events, and to grow in the ability to display Christian attitudes and Christian behaviours during competitive events.

In Quizzing, each child challenges himself or herself to attain an award level. In this approach, children quiz against a base of knowledge, not against each other. Quizzing uses a multiple-choice approach that allows every child to answer every question. Multiple-choice questions offer several answers, and the child chooses the correct one. This approach makes it possible for every child to be a winner.

QUIZZING SUPPLIES

Each child needs Quizzing numbers to answer the questions. Quizzing numbers are four cardboard squares that each have a tab at the top with the numbers 1, 2, 3, and 4 respectively. The numbers fit inside a cardboard box.

You can order cardboard Quizzing boxes and numbers, pictured here, from the Nazarene Publishing House in Kansas City, Missouri, United States of America.

If cardboard Quizzing boxes and numbers are not available in your area, you can make your own Quizzing numbers from paper, paper plates, wood, or whatever you have available. Each child needs a set of Quizzing numbers.

Each group of children will need a person to score their answers. There is a reproducible score sheet on page 140. Use this score sheet to keep track of the answers of each child.

If possible, provide some type of an award for the performance of the children in each Quizzing event. Suggested awards are certificates, stickers, ribbons, trophies, or medals.

Please follow these rules. Competitions that do not operate in accordance with the *Children's Quizzing Official Competition Rules and Procedures* will not qualify for other competition levels.

Children's Quizzing Official Competition Rules and Procedures

AGE AND GRADES

Children in grades 1-6* may participate in Children's Quizzing competitions. Seventh graders, regardless of age, participate in Teen Quizzing.

*For countries other than the United States, grades 1-6 are generally ages 6-12.

BASIC LEVEL COMPETITION

This competition level is for younger or beginning quizzers. Older quizzers who prefer an easier level of competition may also participate in the Basic Level. The questions for the Basic Level are simpler. There are three answers for each question, and there are fifteen questions in each round. The district or regional Children's Quizzing director determines the questions and the number of rounds at each Quizzing competition. Most competitions have two or three rounds.

ADVANCED LEVEL COMPETITION

This competition level is for older quizzers or experienced quizzers. Younger quizzers who want a greater challenge may participate in the Advanced Level. The questions for the Advanced Level are more comprehensive. There are four answers for each question, and there are twenty questions in each round. The district or regional Children's Quizzing director determines the questions and the number of rounds at each Quizzing event.

SWITCHING BETWEEN LEVELS

Children may switch between Basic Level and Advanced Level only for invitational Quizzing competitions. This helps the leaders and the children determine the best level for each child.

For the zone/area, the district, and the regional competitions, the local director must register each child for either Basic Level or Advanced Level. The child must compete at the same level for zone/area, district, and regional competitions.

TYPES OF COMPETITION

Invitational Competition

An invitational competition is between two or more churches. Local Children's Quizzing directors, zone/area Children's Quizzing directors, or district Children's Quizzing directors may organize invitational competitions. Individuals who organize an invitational competition have the responsibility to prepare the competition questions.

Zone/Area Competition

Each district may have smaller groupings of churches that are called zones. If one zone has more quizzers than another zone, the district Children's Quizzing director may separate or combine the zones to create areas with a more equitable distribution of quizzers. The term area means combined or divided zones.

The churches located in each zone/area compete in that zone/area. The district Children's Quizzing director organizes the competition.

Questions for the zone/area competitions are official questions.

E-mail *ChildQuiz@nazarene.org* to request these questions from the General Children's Quizzing Office.

District Competition

Children advance from the zone/area competition to the district competition. The district Children's Quizzing director determines the qualifications for the competition and organizes the competition.

Questions for district competitions are official questions. E-mail *ChildQuiz@nazarene.org* to request these questions from the General Children's Quizzing Office.

Regional Competition

The regional competition is a competition between two or more districts.

When there is a regional Children's Quizzing director, he or she determines the qualifications for the competition and organizes the competition. If there is not a regional director, the participating district directors organize the competition.

Questions for the regional competitions are official questions.

E-mail *ChildQuiz@nazarene.org* to request these questions from the General Children's Quizzing Office.

World Quiz Competition

Every four years, the Children's Ministries International Office sponsors an international World Quiz. Children's Ministries International determines the dates, the locations, the costs, the qualifying dates, and the overall qualifying process for all World Quiz competitions.

E-mail *ChildQuiz@nazarene.org* for more information.

DISTRICT CHILDREN'S QUIZZING DIRECTOR

The district Children's Quizzing director operates all competitions according to the *Children's Quizzing Official Competition Rules and Procedures*. He or she has the authority to introduce additional Quizzing procedures on the district as long as the procedures do not conflict with the *Children's Quizzing Official Competition Rules and Procedures*. The district Children's Quizzing director contacts the General Children's Quizzing Office in Children's Ministries International, when necessary, to request a specific change in the *Children's Quizzing Official Competition Rules and Procedures* for a district. The district Children's Quizzing director makes the decisions and solves the problems within the guidelines of the *Children's Quizzing Official Competition Rules and Procedures*. The district Children's Quizzing director contacts the General Children's Quizzing Office for an official ruling on a specific situation, if necessary.

REGIONAL CHILDREN'S QUIZZING DIRECTOR

The regional Children's Quizzing director creates a regional Children's Quizzing leadership team that consists of all of the district Children's Quizzing directors on the region. The regional Children's Quizzing director remains in contact with this team to keep the procedures consistent across the region. He or she operates and organizes the regional competitions according to the *Children's Quizzing Official Competition Rules and Procedures*. The regional Children's Quizzing director contacts the General Children's Quizzing Office in Children's Ministries International to request any changes in the *Children's Quizzing Official Competition Rules and Procedures* for a specific region. He or she resolves any conflicts that arise with the help of the guidelines of the *Children's Quizzing Official Competition Rules and Procedures*. The regional Children's Quizzing director contacts the General Children's Quizzing Office for an official ruling on a specific situation, if necessary. He or she contacts the General Children's Quizzing Office to place the regional quiz date on the general church calendar.

In the United States and Canada, the regional Children's Quizzing director is a developing position. Currently that person does not preside over district Children's Quizzing directors on the region.

QUIZMASTER

The quizmaster reads the competition questions at a Quizzing competition. The quizmaster reads the question and the multiple-choice answers two times before the children answer the question. He or she follows the *Children's Quizzing Official Competition Rules and Procedures* established by the General Children's Quizzing Office and the district Children's Quizzing director/regional coordinator. In the event of a conflict, the final authority is the district/regional Children's Quizzing director who consults the *Children's Quizzing Official Competition Rules and Procedures*. The quizmaster may participate in discussions with scorekeepers and the district/regional Children's Quizzing director about a challenge. The quizmaster may call a time-out.

SCOREKEEPER

The scorekeeper scores a group of children's answers. He or she may participate in discussions with scorekeepers and the district/regional Children's Quizzing director about a challenge. All scorekeepers are to use the same method and the same symbols to insure correct tabulation of the scores.

OFFICIAL COMPETITION QUESTIONS

The district Children's Quizzing director is the only individual on the district who may obtain a copy of the official zone/area and district competition questions.

The regional Children's Quizzing director is the only individual on the region who may obtain a copy of the official regional competition questions. If there is not a regional Children's Quizzing director, one participating district Children's Quizzing director may obtain a copy of the official regional competition questions.

Order forms for annual official questions will be sent by E-mail each year. Contact the General Children's Quizzing Office at *ChildQuiz@nazarene.org* to update your E-mail address. The official questions will arrive by E-mail to the people who request them.

COMPETITION METHODS

There are two methods of competition.

Individual Method

In the individual method of competition, the children compete as individual children. The score of each child is separate from all other scores. Children from the same church may sit together, but do not add together the individual scores to obtain a church or a team score. There are no bonus questions for individual quizzers.

The individual method is the only method to use for the Basic Level competition.

Combination Method

The combination method combines individual and team Quizzing. In this method, churches may send individual quizzers, the teams, or a combination of these to a competition.

The district Children's Quizzing director determines the number of children needed to form a team. All teams must have the same number of quizzers. The recommended number for a team is four or five children.

The children from the churches that do not have enough quizzers to form a team can compete as individual quizzers.

In the combination method, teams qualify for bonus questions. The bonus points awarded for a correct answer to a bonus question become part of the total score of the team, instead of a score for an individual quizzer. There are bonus questions with the official questions for zone/area, district, and regional competitions. Bonus questions typically involve the recitation of a memory verse.

The district Children's Quizzing director selects either the individual method or the combination method for the Advanced Level of the competition.

TIE SCORES

Ties between individual quizzers or the teams remain as tied scores. All individual children or teams who tie receive the same recognition, the same award, and the same advancement to the next level of competition.

BONUS QUESTIONS

Bonus questions are part of the Advanced Level, but only with teams, not individuals. Teams must qualify for a bonus question. Bonus questions occur after questions 5, 10, 15, and 20.

To qualify for a bonus question, a team may have only as many incorrect answers as there are members on the team. For example, a team of four members may have four or fewer answers that are incorrect. A team of five members may have five or fewer answers that are incorrect.

The bonus points for a correct answer become part of the total score of the team, not of the individual score of a child.

The district Children's Quizzing director determines the way that the children answer bonus questions. In most situations, the child verbally gives the answer to the scorekeeper.

Prior to the reading of the bonus question, the local Children's Quizzing director selects one team member to answer the bonus question. The same child may answer all of the bonus questions in a game, or a different child may answer each bonus question.

TIME-OUTS

The district Children's Quizzing director determines the number of time-outs for each church. Each church receives the same number of time-outs, regardless of the number of individual quizzers or teams from that church. For example, if the district director decides to give one time-out, each church receives one time-out.

The district Children's Quizzing director determines if an automatic time-out will occur during the game and the specific point at which the time-out will occur in each game.

The local Children's Quizzing director is the only individual who may call a time-out for a local church team.

The district Children's Quizzing director or quizmaster may call a time-out at any time.

The district Children's Quizzing director, prior to the start of the competition, determines the length of the time-outs for the competition. All time-outs are to be the same length.

SCORING

There are two methods for scoring. The district Children's Quizzing director selects the method.

Five Points

- Award five points for every correct answer. For example, if a child answers 20 questions correctly in an

Advanced Level round, the child earns a total of 100 points.

- Award five points for every correct bonus answer in an Advanced Level team Quizzing round. For example, if every member of a team with four persons answers 20 questions correctly in an Advanced Level round and the team answers four bonus questions correctly, the team earns a total of 420 points.

Basic Level points will be lower as there are only 15 questions per round, and it is individual competition only.

One Point

Award one point for each correct answer as follows:

- Award one point for every correct answer. For example, if a child answers 20 questions correctly in an Advanced level round, the child earns a total of 20 points.
- Award one point for every correct bonus answer in an Advanced Level team Quizzing round. For example, if every member of a team with four persons answers 20 questions correctly in an Advanced Level round and the team answers four bonus questions correctly, the team earns a total of 84 points.

Basic Level points will be lower as there are only 15 questions per round, and it is individual competition only.

CHALLENGES

Challenges are to be an exception and are not common during a competition.

Request a challenge only when the answer marked as correct in the questions is actually incorrect according to the Bible reference given for that question. Challenges issued for any other reason are invalid.

A quizzer, a Children's Quizzing director, or any other competition participant may not request a challenge because they dislike the wording of a question or answer or think a question is too difficult or confusing.

The local Children's Quizzing director is the only person who may issue a challenge to a competition question.

If an individual other than the local Children's Quizzing director attempts to issue a challenge, the challenge is automatically ruled as "invalid."

Individuals who issue invalid challenges disrupt competition and cause the children to lose their concentration. Individuals who consistently issue invalid challenges or create some problems by arguing about a challenge ruling will lose their privilege of challenging the questions for the remainder of the competition.

The district Children's Quizzing director, or the quizmaster in the absence of the district Children's Quizzing director, has the authority to remove the privilege of challenging questions from any or all individuals who abuse the privilege.

The district Children's Quizzing director determines how to challenge a competition question prior to the start of the competition.

- Will the challenge be written or verbal?
- When can a person challenge (during a game or at the end of a game)?

The district Children's Quizzing director should explain the procedure for the challenges to local Children's Quizzing directors at the beginning of the quiz year.

The quizmaster and district Children's Quizzing director follow these steps to rule the challenge.

- Determine if the challenge is valid or invalid. To do this, listen to the reason for the challenge. If the reason is valid, the answer given as the correct answer is incorrect according to the Bible reference, follow the challenge procedures outlined by the district.

- If the reason for the challenge is invalid, announce that the challenge is invalid, and the competition continues.

If more than one person challenges the same question, the quizmaster or district Children's Quizzing director selects one local quiz director to explain the reason for a challenge. After a question has one challenge, another person may not challenge the same question.

If a challenge is valid, the district Children's Quizzing director, or quizmaster in the director's absence, determines how to handle the challenged question. Select one of the following options.

Option A: Eliminate the question, and do not replace it. The result is that a game of 20 questions becomes a game of 19 questions.

Option B: Give every child the points he or she would receive for a correct answer to the challenged question.

Option C: Replace the challenged question. Ask the quizzers a new question.

Option D: Let the children who gave the answer that was listed as the correct answer in the official questions keep their points. Give another question to the children who gave an answer that was an incorrect answer.

AWARD LEVELS

Children's Quizzing has the philosophy that every child has an opportunity to answer every question, and every child receives recognition for every correct answer he or she gives. Therefore, Children's Quizzing uses multiple-choice competition, and ties are never broken.

Children and churches do not compete against each other. They compete to reach an award level. All of the children and all of the churches who reach the same award level re-

ceive the same award. Ties remain as tied scores.

Recommended Award Levels:
- Bronze Award = 70-79% correct
- Silver Award = 80-89% correct
- Gold Award = 90-99% correct
- Gold All Star = 100% correct

Resolve all scoring and challenge decisions before presenting awards. The quizmaster and scorekeepers should be sure that all final scores are accurate prior to the presentation.

Never take an award from a child after the child receives an award. If there is a mistake, children may receive a higher award but not a lower award. This is true for individual awards and team awards.

COMPETITION ETHICS

The district Children's Quizzing director is the person on the district who has the responsibility to conduct the competitions in accordance with the *Children's Quizzing Official Competition Rules and Procedures.*

1. **Hearing Questions Before the Competition.** Since competitions use the same questions, it is not appropriate for the children and the workers to attend another zone/area, district, or regional competition prior to their participation in their own competition of the same level. If an adult Quizzing worker attends another competition, the district Children's Quizzing director may choose to disqualify the church from participation in their competition. If a parent and/or child attends another competition, the district Children's Quizzing director may choose to disqualify the church from participation in their competition.

2. Worker's Conduct and Attitudes. Adults are to conduct themselves in a professional and in a Christian manner. The discussions about disagreements with the district Children's Quizzing director, quizmaster, or scorekeepers are to be private. Adult Quizzing workers should not share information about the disagreement with the children. A cooperative spirit and good sportsmanship are important. The decisions and the rulings of the district Children's Quizzing director are final. Relay these decisions in a positive tone to the children and to the adults.

CHEATING

Any cheating is serious. Treat the cheating seriously.

The district Children's Quizzing director, in discussion with the district Children's Ministries Council, determines the policy to follow in the event that a child or an adult cheats during a competition.

Make sure that all local children's ministries directors, children's pastors, and local Children's Quizzing directors receive the policy and the procedures of the district.

Before accusing an adult or a child of cheating, have some evidence or a witness that the cheating occurred.

Ensure that the quiz continues and that the person accused of cheating does not suffer embarrassment in front of other people. Here is a sample procedure.

- If you suspect that a child cheated, ask someone to serve as a judge to watch the areas, but do not point out any child whom you suspect. After a few questions, ask the opinion of the judge. If the judge did not see any cheating, continue with the quiz.
- If the judge saw a child who was cheating, ask the judge to affirm it. Do not act until everyone is sure.
- Explain the problem to the local Children's Quizzing director, and ask the director to talk with the accused person privately.
- The quizmaster, the judge, and the local Children's Quizzing director should watch for continued cheating.
- If the cheating continues, the quizmaster and the local Children's Quizzing director should talk with the accused person privately.
- If the cheating continues, the quizmaster should tell the local Children's Quizzing director that he or she will eliminate the score of the child from official competition.
- In the case that a scorekeeper cheated, the district Children's Quizzing director will ask the scorekeeper to leave, and a new scorekeeper will take his or her place.
- In the case that someone in the audience cheated, the district Children's Quizzing director will handle the situation in the most appropriate manner.

UNRESOLVED DECISIONS

Consult with the General Children's Quizzing Office regarding unresolved decisions.

one Matthew 1:18–2:23

Memory Verse

"'She will give birth to a son, and you are to give him the name Jesus, because he will save his people from their sins'" (Matthew 1:21).

Biblical Truth

Jesus is God the Son, the Saviour that God promised to us.

Focus

In this study, the children will learn that God keeps his promises.

Teaching Tips

As you lead the Bible study, remind the students that Jesus is God's Son. He is fully God and fully human. In this study a virgin is an unmarried woman.

BIBLICAL COMMENTARY

Many times in the Old Testament, God asked his people to remember what he taught them and what he did for them. God desired that what they learned from the history of their interactions with him would guide their lives. The people learned that God is consistent, both in his actions and in his character.

If a prophet claimed to be sent from God but the message of the prophet was not consistent with what they learned about God, that prophet was false. Therefore, it was very important for Matthew to tell the Jewish-Christian community that Jesus fulfilled Old Testament prophecies. Jesus was the promised Messiah and his mission was a continuation of God's plan.

What does it mean that Jesus fulfilled those prophecies? The fact that Jesus' life paralleled previous events in salvation history (like the Exodus) was remarkable proof that God was personally involved.

CHARACTERISTICS OF GOD

- God sent his Son, Jesus, to save us from our sins.
- God keeps his promises.

PEOPLE

Holy Spirit is the Spirit of God.
Jesus is God's only Son, the Saviour of the world.
Jesus is fully God and fully human.

The **Magi** were wise men from the East who came to visit Jesus.

King Herod was the king of Judea at the time of the birth of Jesus.

A **prophet** is someone whom God has chosen to receive and to give special messages from him.

PLACES

Bethlehem is the city where the birth of Jesus occurred.

Jerusalem is the main city where the Jews went to worship.

Nazareth is the town in Galilee where Jesus lived.

THINGS

Frankincense is a sweet-smelling substance that a person burned as an offering to God.

Myrrh is a liquid that people used in oil, in perfume, and for preparing bodies for burial.

ACTIVITY

Before class, designate clear boundaries in the area (indoors or outdoors).

Choose three children who will be the "Magi." Explain that at the time of the birth of Jesus, Magi were wise men from the East. In this game, the "Magi" will close or cover their eyes and count to 50. While the "Magi" count, the other players scatter and find some places to hide. The "Magi" will then search for the children. The last three children whom the "Magi" find will become the new "Magi." If time permits, play this game until every child has the opportunity to be one of the "Magi."

Say, **Today we will learn about some Magi who searched for a special gift.**

BIBLICAL LESSON

Prepare the following story, adapted from Matthew 1:18--2:23 before you tell it to the children.

Mary and Joseph announced publicly that they would marry. Before their marriage, Mary realized she was "with child through the Holy Spirit."

Joseph wanted to divorce her quietly. However, an angel appeared to Joseph in a dream. The angel said, "Joseph son of David, do not be afraid to take Mary home as your wife. She will give birth to a son, and you are to give him the name Jesus, because he will save his people from their sins.

This fulfilled what the Lord said through the prophet: "'The virgin will be with child and will give birth to a son, and they will call him Immanuel'--which means, 'God with us.'"

Joseph awoke and did what the angel said. When Mary gave birth to the child, Joseph named the baby Jesus.

After the birth of Jesus in Bethlehem in Judea, Magi from the East came to Jerusalem to worship the newborn King of the Jews. The Magi asked the king, "Where is

the one who was born king of the Jews? We saw his star in the east and came to worship him."

When King Herod heard about this, he became disturbed. The chief priests and teachers of the Law said that the birth of the baby would happen in Bethlehem. King Herod asked the Magi to tell him when and where they found the Christ child.

The Magi followed the star until it stopped over the place where the child lived. When the Magi saw the child, they bowed down and worshiped him. Then they presented to Jesus their gifts of gold, frankincense, and myrrh. However, God warned them in a dream not to go back to King Herod. So they returned to their country by another route.

After the Magi left, an angel of the Lord appeared to Joseph in a dream. The angel told Joseph to take the child and his mother and to escape to Egypt. Joseph did what the angel said. They stayed in Egypt until King Herod died.

When King Herod heard what the Magi did, he was extremely angry. He gave the orders to kill in Bethlehem and in the surrounding areas all of the boys who were two years old or younger.

After King Herod died, an angel appeared to Joseph again and told him to take the child and his mother to Israel. Joseph did this. God gave to Joseph another warning in a dream. So, Joseph and his family moved to the district of Galilee, to the town of Nazareth. This fulfilled the words of the prophet that Jesus was a Nazarene.

Encourage the children to answer the following questions. There are no right or wrong answers. These questions will help the children to understand the story and to apply it to their lives.

1. Has someone ever promised you something? Did that person keep the promise? How do you feel about a person who does not keep a promise?

2. Jesus is fully God and fully human. How is this statement true? How does this affect our lives?

3. Do you think it took courage and faith for Joseph to follow the instruction of the angels? Why or why not?

4. Why did King Herod want Jesus to die?

5. How does the memory verse, Matthew 1:21, relate to this story? How does this verse give you hope?

Say, Think about a promise someone made to you. Did you wait a long time to receive what the person promised to you? God promised to send to his people a Messiah—a Saviour. They waited a long time for this Messiah to come.

Israel expected their Messiah to come as a king who would save them from their enemies. Instead, God sent them the promised Messiah as a baby—a baby who was both God and man. Jesus is God, the Son.

MEMORY VERSE

Practice the study's memory verse. You will find suggestions for Memory Verse Activities on pages 137-138.

ADDITIONAL ACTIVITIES

Choose from any of these options to enhance the children's Bible study.

1. Say, **Pretend that you are one of the Magi. Would you listen to King Herod or to God?** Make a chart to compare the advantages and disadvantages of each decision.

2. Encourage the children to imagine the trip to Egypt with Mary and Joseph. Jesus was very young, and the family had to travel a long distance to keep Jesus safe. Use a map and map scale to calculate how far that Mary and Joseph travelled. Create a display to illustrate the things that Mary and Joseph needed on their journey.

QUESTIONS FOR BASIC COMPETITION

To prepare the children for competition, read Matthew 1:18--2:23 to them.

1 Who pledged to marry Joseph? (1:18)
  1. Elizabeth
  2. Mary
  3. Rachel

2 What did an angel tell Joseph to do when he thought he would divorce Mary? (1:19-20)
  1. To take her home as his wife
  2. To divorce her quietly
  3. To marry her secretly

3 Why was Joseph to name the baby Jesus? (1:21)
  1. It was a good name in his family.
  2. Jesus would save his people from their sins.
  3. All of the important people had the name of Jesus.

4 After the birth of Jesus, who came from the East to Jerusalem? (2:1)
  1. The Magi
  2. King Herod
  3. Some of the cousins of Jesus

5 Why had the Magi come from the East? (2:2)
  1. To worship King Herod
  2. To worship Mary and Joseph
  3. To worship the newly born king of the Jews

6 What did the Magi do when they saw Jesus? (2:11)
  1. They bowed down and worshiped him.
  2. The presented him with gifts.
  3. Both answers are correct.

7 Who searched for the child (Jesus) to kill him? (2:13)
  1. The Pharaoh of Egypt
  2. King Herod
  3. The king of Persia

8 How long did Mary, Joseph, and Jesus stay in Egypt? (2:15)
  1. Until Jesus was 12 years old
  2. Until Joseph died
  3. Until the death of King Herod

9 After King Herod died, what did an angel tell Joseph to do? (2:19-20)
  1. "Take the child and his mother to Israel."
  2. "Take the child and his mother to Bethlehem."
  3. "Take the child and his mother to the Temple."

10 How did the prophets say that people would describe Jesus? (2:23)
  1. A miracle-worker
  2. A Nazarene
  3. The greatest man who lived

QUESTIONS FOR ADVANCED COMPETITION

To prepare the children for competition, read Matthew 1:18--2:23 to them.

1 What happened before Mary and Joseph married? (1:18)
1. Mary decided not to marry Joseph.
2. Joseph secretly married another girl.
3. The parents of Mary stopped the relationship.
4. **Mary was with child through the Holy Spirit.**

2 What kind of man was Joseph? (1:19)
1. Arrogant
2. Sinful
3. An important businessman in Nazareth
4. **Righteous**

3 What did Joseph name the baby? (1:25)
1. **Jesus**
2. Joseph
3. John
4. Moses

4 When King Herod heard what the Magi said, what did he do? (2:4, 7)
1. He called together the chief priests and teachers of the Law.
2. He asked the priests and teachers where the birth of Christ would happen.
3. He secretly met with the Magi, and he asked them when the star appeared.
4. **All of the above**

5 Why did the Magi return to their home by another route, rather than to report to King Herod? (2:12)
1. They wanted to return home more quickly.
2. **They were warned in a dream not to go to Herod.**
3. They wanted to see other parts of the world.
4. They forgot to report to Herod.

6 After the Magi left, what did the angel of the Lord tell Joseph? (2:13)
1. Take the child and his mother to Egypt.
2. Stay in Egypt until God told him to return.
3. King Herod would search for Jesus to kill him.
4. **All of the above**

7 When King Herod learned that the Magi tricked him, what did he do? (2:16)
1. He went to Bethlehem by himself.
2. He sent soldiers to capture the Magi.
3. **He gave orders to kill in and near Bethlehem all of the boys who were two years old or younger.**
4. He went to Egypt to find Jesus.

8 What happened after Herod died? (2:19-20)
1. **An angel told Joseph to return to Israel with Mary and Jesus.**
2. A king in Egypt tried to find and to kill Jesus.
3. Mary and Joseph decided to stay in Egypt permanently.
4. Some prophets came to visit Jesus in Egypt.

9 How did Mary, Joseph, and Jesus fulfil a prophecy when they went to Nazareth? (2:23)
1. All true prophets came from Nazareth.
2. **People would call Jesus a Nazarene.**
3. Jesus would have a happy childhood in Nazareth.
4. All of the above

10 Finish this verse: "'She will give birth to a son, and you are to give him the name Jesus, because . . .'" (Matthew 1:21)
1. **"'. . . he will save his people from their sins.'"**
2. "'. . . I command this.'"
3. "'. . . that is what the prophets said to name him.'"
4. "'. . . it is a good name.'"

STUDY two Matthew 3:1—4:12, 17-25

Memory Verse

"Jesus answered, 'It is written: "Man does not live on bread alone, but on every word that comes from the mouth of God"'" (Matthew 4:4).

Biblical Truth

Jesus used the Word of God to defeat temptation.

Focus

In this study, the children will learn about John the Baptist. He taught the people to repent and to prepare for the arrival of the Messiah. John baptized Jesus. After this event, Satan tempted Jesus in the wilderness. As Jesus walked beside the Sea of Galilee, he called the first of his disciples.

Teaching Tip

As you lead the Bible study, focus on what it means to be a disciple of Jesus.

BIBLICAL COMMENTARY

God's Word plays a part in the way people behave, whether they are righteous or wicked. In this study, we will learn how that is possible.

John the Baptist fulfilled the prophecy of Isaiah about the herald of God. The writing of Matthew shows that God, who was at work in the Old Testament, was still at work in New Testament times.

The Pharisees and Sadducees were expert scholars of the Law, but John rebuked them. They interpreted poorly the Scripture. Many Jews followed their teachings. So the Pharisees and Sadducees led the people away from God.

While Jesus was in the wilderness, Satan quoted scripture to Jesus to tempt Jesus to sin. However, Jesus quoted scripture in response to Satan. Old Testament teachings still help us to know God and his will for our lives. When we have temptations, we can resist them when we use the guidance from the Scripture.

We must approach the Bible with the right attitude. We must understand what we read and apply the message properly.

CHARACTERISTICS OF GOD

- God sends the Holy Spirit to us to help us.
- God helps us to resist temptation.

WORDS OF OUR FAITH

The **Holy Spirit** is the Spirit of God. The Holy Spirit

empowers us to live for God when we trust in Jesus as our Saviour.

PEOPLE

The **Pharisees** were a Jewish religious group who followed strictly the Law of Moses. They added many other rules and customs to the Law.

The **Sadducees** were Jewish leaders from families of priests who believed only in following the Law of Moses. They did not believe in the resurrection of the dead or in angels.

THINGS

Baptism is a public ceremony that symbolizes a person's rebirth in Christ.

To **fast** is to give up something, usually food, for a time. A person does this and uses the time to pray and focus on God.

To **repent** is to turn away from the sin and to turn to God.

Temptation is the desire to do something you know you should not do.

ACTIVITY

You will need these items for this activity:
- A blindfold
- Some chairs or other items to use as some obstacles
- A roll of tape

Before class, place the obstacles around the room. Plan a route that a child will take around or through the obstacles. Mark the path on the ground with the tape.

Select a volunteer. Tell the volunteer to step outside the room. While the volunteer is outside, say to the other children, **Today we will learn how the Word of God helps us to avoid temptations. I will give instructions to the volunteer who will wear a blindfold. While I give instructions, the rest of you will shout incorrect instructions to the volunteer. Try to lead him or her from the right path.**

Bring the volunteer back into the room. Place the volunteer at the beginning of the path, and place the blindfold across the eyes of the child. Say, **I will give to you some instructions on how to navigate the path. Listen to my voice only!**

Guide the child with a normal speaking voice. The volunteer should follow your instructions and reach the end of the path. Repeat the activity with other volunteers, if time permits.

Say, **God gives us instructions through the Bible. When we study the Bible, we learn how to avoid temptations. Today, we will learn about a time when Satan tempted Jesus.**

BIBLICAL LESSON

Prepare the following story, adapted from Matthew 3:1 - 4:12, 17-25 before you tell it to the children.

John the Baptist began to preach in the desert. He said, "Repent, for the kingdom of heaven is near." John fulfilled the proph-

ecy of Isaiah that someone would preach in the desert and would prepare the way for Jesus.

John wore clothes made from camel's hair. He also wore a leather belt. He ate locusts and wild honey. People came from far away to see John. After they listened to John, many repented of their sins. John baptized these people.

When John saw the Pharisees and the Sadducees, he said, "You brood of vipers! Show that you repent from your sins. You are descended from Abraham, but that lineage will not save you. God can make children for Abraham from stones. Every tree that does not produce good fruit will be cut down and thrown in the fire."

John said, "I baptize people with water. However, someone else will come after me. He will baptize you with the Holy Spirit."

Jesus came to John, and he wanted John to baptize him. John said to Jesus, "You should baptize me. Why do you come to me?"

Jesus said, "This is the right thing for me to do."

When John baptized Jesus, the Spirit of God descended from heaven as a dove. The dove landed on Jesus. A voice from the heaven said, "This is my Son, whom I love; with him I am well pleased."

After John baptized Jesus, Jesus went into the desert. Jesus fasted for forty days and forty nights, and he became hungry. Satan came to Jesus, and he said, "If you are the Son of God, tell these stones to become bread."

Jesus answered, "It is written, 'Man does not live on bread alone, but on every word that comes from the mouth of God.'"

Satan took Jesus to Jerusalem, and they went to the highest place on the top of the temple. Satan said, "If you are the son of God, jump off of the temple. It is written that God will send his angels to protect you."

Jesus said, "It is also written: 'Do not put the Lord your God to the test.'"

Then Satan took Jesus to a high mountain and showed him all of the kingdoms of the world. Satan said, "Bow down and worship me, and I will give you all of the kingdoms of the world."

Jesus said, "Get away from me, Satan! It is written: 'Worship the Lord your God, and serve him only.'" Satan went away, and the angels came and cared for Jesus.

Jesus heard that John was in prison, so Jesus went back to Galilee. As he walked, he saw two brothers, Simon, named Peter, and Andrew. They used nets to catch fish. Jesus said, "Come and follow me. You will catch men instead of fish." They left their nets, and they followed Jesus.

Jesus saw two more brothers. Their names were James and John. These men were the sons of Zebedee. They were fishermen. Jesus called to them, and they left their nets to follow him.

Jesus went throughout Galilee. He taught in the synagogues, and he preached to the people. He also healed sick people. News about Jesus spread into Syria, and the people of Syria brought their sick people to Jesus. They also brought people who were possessed with demons and some who were paralyzed. Jesus healed all of them. Large crowds gathered around Jesus wherever he went.

Encourage the children to answer the following questions. There are no right or wrong answers. These questions help the children to understand the story and to apply it to their lives.

1. **How do you think that John the Baptist felt when he baptized Jesus?**
2. **Why was Jesus tempted? What are some temptations you have experienced in your life?**
3. **Why do you think that Jesus chose Simon Peter, Andrew, James, and John to be his disciples?**

Say, **It was difficult for Jesus to be in the desert. The sun was extremely hot. Jesus fasted for forty days and for forty nights, and this made him very hungry.**

Satan tempted Jesus in three different ways. However, Jesus resisted the temptations of Satan. Jesus displayed for us how to use the Scripture to defend against temptation. We can use the Scripture when Satan tempts us.

MEMORY VERSE

Practice the study's memory verse. You will find suggestions for Memory Verse Activities on pages 137-138.

ADDITIONAL ACTIVITIES

Choose from these options to enhance the children's Bible study.

1. Read Matthew 3:13-17. Using crayons, markers, or pencils, tell each student to draw a picture of the baptism of Jesus. As a class, discuss the different events that happened when John baptized Jesus.

2. As a class, write some temptations that the children face. Then, read 1 Corinthians 10:13. Write this verse on a large banner where the class will see it every day. Thank God for his promise to "not let you be tempted beyond what you can bear." Let the children decorate the banner.

QUESTIONS FOR BASIC COMPETITION

To prepare the children for competition, read Matthew 3:1--4:12, 17-25 to them.

1 Who preached in the Desert of Judea? (3:1)
1. James, the brother of Jesus
2. Joseph
3. **John the Baptist**

2 What was the message of John the Baptist? (3:2)
1. **"Repent, for the kingdom of heaven is near."**
2. "Repent, or you will die tomorrow."
3. "Jesus is the Saviour. Trust him."

3 What did the prophet Isaiah foretell about John the Baptist? (3:3)
1. John would be a voice calling in the desert.
2. John would say, "Prepare the way for the Lord."
3. **Both answers are correct.**

4 Who came from Galilee for baptism by John the Baptist? (3:13)
1. The Pharisees
2. **Jesus**
3. All of John's relatives

5 What happened when John baptized Jesus? (3:16)
1. Heaven opened.
2. The Spirit of God descended like a dove.
3. **Both answers are correct.**

6 How long did Jesus fast before Satan tempted him? (4:2)
1. 30 days and 30 nights
2. **40 days and 40 nights**
3. 40 days and 30 nights

7 What did Jesus say when Satan tempted him to throw himself off the temple? (4:7)
1. **"'Do not put the Lord your God to the test.'"**
2. "'I am afraid.'"
3. "'I cannot be tempted.'"

8 What did Satan promise to Jesus if Jesus would bow down and worship him? (4:8-9)
1. All of the kingdom of King Herod
2. The kingdom of Jerusalem
3. **All of the kingdoms of the world**

9 What did Jesus say when he called to Peter and to Andrew? (4:19)
1. **"'I will make you fishers of men.'"**
2. "'I will make you my disciples.'"
3. "'I will make you strong.'"

10 Where did Jesus go to teach, to preach, and to heal every disease? (4:23)
1. Throughout Jericho
2. Throughout Egypt
3. **Throughout Galilee**

QUESTIONS FOR ADVANCED COMPETITION

To prepare the children for competition, read Matthew 3:1--4:12, 17-25 to them.

1 Where did John the Baptist preach? (3:1)
1. On the banks of the Jerusalem River
2. In the temple in Jerusalem
3. In the Desert of Judea
4. In Egypt

2 What did John the Baptist eat? (3:4)
1. Locusts and wild boar
2. Wild honey and honeycomb
3. Locusts and wild honey
4. Locusts and wildflowers

3 What did Jesus say to John before John baptized him? (3:15)
1. "'It is proper to do this; God commanded it.'"
2. "'If you don't do this, no one will.'"
3. "'This is the way for my baptism to happen.'
4. "'It is proper for us to do this to fulfil all righteousness.'"

4 After John baptized Jesus, what did a voice from heaven say? (3:17)
1. "This is my Son, whom I love; with him I am well pleased."
2. "This is my Son, the Saviour."
3. "This is my Son; treat him rightly."
4. "This is Jesus Christ, Son of the living God."

5 Who led Jesus into the desert? (4:1)
1. Jesus himself
2. The devil
3. The Spirit
4. John the Baptist

6 What happened to Jesus after the devil left? (4:11)
1. Some angels came, and they tempted Jesus.
2. Some angels came and they attended to him.
3. The devil came back to tempt Jesus again.
4. God comforted Jesus.

7 Whom did Jesus see as he walked beside the Sea of Galilee? (4:18)
1. Philip and Nathanael
2. Judas and James
3. Peter and Andrew
4. Bartholomew and Judas

8 What did James and John do when Jesus asked them to follow Him? (4:21-22)
1. They left their nets and their father, and they followed Jesus.
2. They talked to Peter and Andrew, and then they followed Jesus.
3. They asked the permission of Zebedee to follow Jesus.
4. They refused to follow Jesus.

9 As news about Jesus spread throughout Syria, whom did the people bring to him? (4:24)
1. All who were ill with various diseases
2. People who suffered from severe pain
3. People who were demon-possessed and people who were paralyzed
4. All of the above

10 Finish this verse: "Jesus answered, 'It is written: "Man does not live on bread alone..."'" (Matthew 4:4)
1. "'"...but on every commandment of the Lord on high."'"
2. "'"...but on every word I have spoken to him."'"
3. "'"...but on every word that comes from the mouth of God."'"
4. "'"...but on all the law and the prophets."'"

three Matthew 5:1-37

Memory Verse

"'Blessed are the poor in spirit, for theirs is the kingdom of heaven. Blessed are those who mourn, for they will be comforted. Blessed are the meek, for they will inherit the earth. Blessed are those who hunger and thirst for righteousness, for they will be filled'" (Matthew 5:3-6).

Biblical Truth

Jesus teaches us how to live out God's commands as members of his kingdom.

Focus

In this study, children will learn that Jesus taught new ways to understand and obey God's laws about murder, adultery, divorce, and oaths.

Teaching Tips

Your students may have questions about the section on divorce. Help students to understand that Jesus came to transform legalistic thinking regarding all aspects of the law, including divorce. Jesus demonstrated that fostering love and relationship is the purpose of God's law.

BIBLICAL COMMENTARY

In the Sermon on the Mount, Jesus explained that he came to bring the Law and the Prophets to their completeness. The Law and the Prophets were like half-full vessels, and Jesus finished the lessons they started. Some of the teachings of Jesus seemed contrary to Old Testament Scripture. However, the teachings of Jesus were consistent with the Old Testament. Jesus surprised many of those who listened to him. They received new insight into God's intention for humanity, and they also had to correct a number of false teachings of the Pharisees and Sadducees.

The purpose of the Law was to teach Israel about God's character and values. The Law also taught them how to live a holy life. The Law helped them to realize the value of a relationship with God and their need for forgiveness. Many people misunderstood the Law. They believed it was sufficient to practice certain behaviours without changing their character. Jesus taught the people to internalize the Law. Jesus applied the Law to our hearts--our character, desires, attitudes, and ways of thinking--in addition to our behaviour.

CHARACTERISTICS OF GOD

- Jesus teaches us how to live as members of his kingdom.
- Jesus teaches us to obey God's laws because we love him.

WORDS OF OUR FAITH

The Kingdom of Heaven is wherever God rules. We see the **kingdom of heaven** best where people worship and obey Him as Lord of their lives.

ACTIVITY

You will need these items for this activity:
- Some flashlights
- A large bowl

Turn off the lights in the room. Say, **Can you see anything in the dark?** Turn on a flashlight, but put it under the bowl. Set the bowl on the floor or the table so that only a small amount of light shows underneath it. Say, **What can you see?** Remove the bowl, and discuss what the children see with the light.

Say, **When we obey Jesus, the people can "see" what Jesus is like through our actions. It is similar to the light. When the room was dark, or when the flashlight was under a bowl, it was difficult to see in the room. When I took the bowl off of the flashlight, we saw many things in the room. We should not hide our light or feel embarrassed to share the love of Jesus with others! Jesus wants our "light" to shine for him so that others can see what he is like.**

Option: Give each child a flashlight, and have the children turn on the flashlights when you say the word, **"Light."** If you want to do this option, you could ask students to bring a flashlight from their home for the lesson.

BIBLICAL LESSON

Prepare the following story, adapted from Matthew 5:1-37 before you tell it to the children.

Jesus looked around him and saw the crowds. He went up the mountain, and he sat down. The disciples followed him. Jesus began to teach the people how God wants us to live.

"Blessed are the poor in spirit, for theirs is the kingdom of heaven.

Blessed are those who mourn, for they will be comforted.

Blessed are the meek, for they will inherit the earth.

Blessed are those who hunger and thirst for righteousness, for they will be filled.

Blessed are the merciful, for they will be shown mercy.

Blessed are the pure in heart, for they will see God.

Blessed are the peacemakers, for they will be called sons of God.

Blessed are those who are persecuted because of righteousness, for theirs is the kingdom of heaven.

Blessed are you when people insult you, persecute you and falsely say all kinds of evil against you because of me.

Rejoice and be glad, because great is your reward in heaven."

Jesus taught that the believers need

to live so that the people see the love of God through them.

Then Jesus said, "You are the salt of the earth. But if the salt loses its saltiness, how can it be made salty again? It is no longer good for anything. . . You are the light of the world. A city on the hill cannot be hidden. People do not light a lamp and put it under a bowl. They put it on a stand, and it gives light to everyone in the house. In the same way, let your light shine before men, that they may see your good deeds and praise your Father in heaven."

Some people thought that Jesus would throw out the Old Testament laws and teachings. Jesus said, "I have not come to do away with the Law or the Prophets. I have come to fulfil them. Whoever practices and teaches these commands will be called great in the kingdom of heaven."

Jesus clarified the meaning of the laws of God. "You have heard that it was said to the people long ago, 'Do not murder.' But I tell you that anyone who is angry with his brother will be subject to judgment."

Jesus said, "You have heard that it was said, 'Do not commit adultery.' But I tell you that anyone who looks at a woman lustfully has already committed adultery with her in his heart."

Jesus said, "You have heard that it was said to the people long ago, 'Do not break your oath, but keep the oaths you have made to the Lord.' "But I tell you,

Do not swear at all, either by heaven, by the earth, by Jerusalem, or by your head. Simply let your 'Yes' be 'Yes', and your 'No,' 'No.'"

Encourage the children to answer the following questions. There are no right or wrong answers. These questions will help the children to understand the story and to apply it to their lives.

1. Jesus spoke to his disciples and probably to many others. How do you think the people felt about the new ideas that Jesus taught?

2. How were the teachings of Jesus different from the Old Testament teachings?

Say, **God gives us commands, and he wants us to obey them. Some people obey, but they grumble about it. In his Sermon on the Mount, Jesus taught about obeying the commands of God because we love him. Jesus taught us to obey with our outward behaviour and with our heart and attitude. God sees what is in the hearts of people. Choose to obey God with a willing and positive attitude. This is what it means to be a member of his kingdom.**

MEMORY VERSE

Practice the study's memory verse. You will find suggestions for Memory Verse Activities on pages 137-138.

ADDITIONAL ACTIVITIES

Choose from any of these options to enhance the children's Bible study.

1. Write the word *blessed* on construction paper. Think about these questions: **Who is blessed? Why are they blessed? What does this word mean?** Ask these questions to your family members and friends. Write the responses randomly on the construction paper.

2. Research the Old Testament laws that coordinate with the things Jesus taught in the Sermon on the Mount. What were some ways the Israelites practiced these laws in the Old Testament? On a poster, create two columns. In one column, write the information you researched from the Old Testament. In the other column, write the new ideas Jesus taught about each law.

QUESTIONS FOR BASIC COMPETITION

To prepare the children for competition, read Matthew 5:1-37 to them.

1 When Jesus saw the crowds, what did he do? (5:1)
  1. **He went up on the mountain, and he sat down.**
  2. He went to the next city.
  3. Both answers are correct.

2 What did Jesus begin to do on the mountainside? (5:2)
  1. To sing
  2. **To teach**
  3. To pray

3 Why are the poor in spirit blessed? (5:3)
  1. **"Theirs is the kingdom of heaven."**
  2. "They will receive mercy."
  3. "They will inherit the earth."

4 Who did Jesus say would inherit the earth? (5:5)
  1. The poor in spirit
  2. **The meek**
  3. The merciful

5 What did Jesus say that we should call the peacemakers? (5:9)
  1. Peaceful people
  2. Sons of heaven
  3. **Sons of God**

6 According to Jesus, why should persecuted people rejoice and be glad? (5:11-12)
  1. Great is their reward in heaven.
  2. This is the way that people treated the prophets.
  3. **Both answers are correct.**

7 What happens when a person lets his or her light shine before the people? (5:16)
  1. Rooms become brighter.
  2. **People praise the Father in heaven.**
  3. The city is in darkness.

8 What did Jesus say that he had come to fulfil? (5:17)
  1. The Ten Commandments
  2. **The Law and the Prophets**
  3. The Beatitudes

9 What did Jesus say about oaths? (5:34)
  1. "Do not keep the oaths that you make."
  2. **"Do not swear an oath at all."**
  3. "Be careful about the oaths that you make."

10 What did Jesus say that people should do instead of an oath? (5:37)
  1. **"Let your 'Yes' be 'Yes,' and your 'No,' 'No.'"**
  2. Never make a promise to anyone.
  3. Shake hands to show that you will keep your word.

QUESTIONS FOR ADVANCED COMPETITION

To prepare the children for competition, read Matthew 5:1-37 to them.

1 Who did Jesus say would receive comfort? (5:4)
1. Those who are sick
2. **Those who mourn**
3. Those in great pain
4. All who suffer from persecution

2 What will happen to those who hunger and thirst for righteousness? (5:6)
1. **They will be filled.**
2. They will give to others.
3. Many will be taken from them.
4. Their hearts will find rest.

3 What happens to the pure in heart? (5:8)
1. People will treat them in nice ways.
2. They will receive many things.
3. **They will see God.**
4. They will be full of joy.

4 What did Jesus tell those who endure persecution to do? (5:11-12)
1. **"Rejoice and be glad."**
2. "Ask others for much help."
3. "Be very sad about what happened."
4. "Fight any person who hurts you."

5 To what did Jesus compare the people of God? (5:13)
1. Basil
2. **Salt**
3. Pepper
4. Garlic powder

6 Why did Jesus say, "'Let your light shine before men'"? (5:16)
1. "To give light to everyone in the house"
2. **"That they may see your good deeds and praise your Father in heaven"**
3. "So that a city on a hill will shine brightly"
4. All of the above

7 Who came to fulfil the Law and the Prophets (5:17)
1. Moses
2. Joshua
3. The Pharisees
4. **Jesus**

8 To what was a person answerable when he or she said to a brother, "Raca"? (5:22)
1. The Roman courts
2. **The Sanhedrin**
3. The synagogue
4. All of the above

9 If a person offers a gift at the altar and remembers that a brother has something against him or her, what should the person do? (5:23-25)
1. Leave the gift in front of the altar.
2. Go and reconcile with the brother.
3. Come and offer the gift.
4. **All of the above**

10 Finish this verse: "Blessed are the poor in spirit, for theirs is the kingdom of heaven. Blessed are those who mourn, for they will be comforted. Blessed are the meek, for they will inherit the earth. Blessed are those who hunger . . ." (5:3-6)
1. ". . . to be good, for they will be called the people of God."
2. " . . . for God's love, for God's blessing will rest on them."
3. **". . . and thirst for righteousness, for they will be filled."**
4. "'. . . and eat their fill, for they will never go hungry.'"

four

Matthew 5:38--6:34

Memory Verse

"'Blessed are the merciful, for they will be shown mercy. Blessed are the pure in heart, for they will see God. Blessed are the peacemakers, for they will be called sons of God. Blessed are those who are persecuted because of righteousness, for theirs is the kingdom of heaven'" (Matthew 5:7-10).

Biblical Truth

Jesus teaches us how to live a righteous life.

Focus

This lesson will help the children to learn that Jesus taught us how to live a righteous life. We should avoid revenge, love our enemies, and give to the people in need.

Teaching Tips

As you lead the Bible study, focus on the practical ways that Jesus taught the people to live as members of God's kingdom.

BIBLICAL COMMENTARY

In the Old Testament, "an eye for eye" taught the Israelites about justice. The punishment for a crime should equal the severity of the crime. It helped the Israelites to understand the just character of God. It taught God's standards of right and wrong. The wicked were not to abuse the righteous and the weak. It protected the criminals from a punishment that was too harsh.

When Jesus was on earth, "eye for eye" was a justification for personal revenge. Jesus corrected this view. A strike on the right cheek was a major insult. To turn the other cheek was to accept the insult. An insult was not a legal issue that the courts decided. It was a petty occurrence outside of the law.

Jesus spoke about other instances of justice. For instance, if someone sues you for a wrong you committed, pay back more than you owe. When someone asks you to do something you do not want to do, do extra work for that job. Do not help people and expect something in return. The truly righteous person is generous and puts love above personal conflicts and inconveniences.

CHARACTERISTICS OF GOD

- God is righteous.
- God wants us to seek his kingdom and to trust him.

34

FAITH WORDS

Righteousness is a right relationship with God. To be righteous means to obey God because of your relationship with him. A righteous person is right or good in the thoughts, the words, and the actions.

PEOPLE

Pagans were the people who worshipped the idols instead of God.

PLACES

The **synagogue** was a place where Jews met to read the Scripture and to worship God.

THINGS

A **cloak** was a long piece of clothing. It was a robe during the day and a blanket at night.

A **tunic** was the main piece of clothing that the men wore.

Prayer is a conversation with God that includes both talking and listening.

To **fast** is to give up something, usually food, for a time in order to pray and focus on God.

ACTIVITY

You will need these items for this activity:

- Two large pieces of blank paper
- Some coloured markers or some crayons

Before class, post the pieces of the paper on the wall of the classroom. On one piece of the paper, draw a picture of a sparrow (or another type of a bird). On the other piece of the paper, draw a picture of a lily (or another type of a flower).

Say, **Today, we will choose colours for this bird and for this flower. When I ask for a colour, raise your hand. When I point to you, tell me what part of the picture to colour.**

As you colour the pictures, try to call on each child before you finish the picture. When you complete the picture, leave it in the classroom for everyone to see.

Say, **We coloured these pictures of a sparrow and of a lily. However, God made the sparrow and the lily more beautiful than we ever could make them. Today we will learn that God cares for us even more than he does for these beautiful things.**

BIBLICAL LESSON

Prepare the following story, adapted from Matthew 5:38--6:34, before you tell it to the children.

Jesus continued to speak to the people who gathered around him. Jesus taught the people how to treat the people who mistreated them. Jesus said, "You have heard it said, 'Eye for eye, and tooth for tooth' However, I have a new instruction for you. When someone does an evil thing to you, do not resist it. If he or she hits

you on the right cheek, allow him or her to hit your left cheek as well. If someone tries to take your tunic, give to them your cloak as well. If someone forces you to walk one mile with them, walk two miles instead. Give to the people who ask you for something. Do not refuse people who need something."

"Some people say to love your neighbour and hate your enemy. But I tell you: Love your enemies and pray for those who persecute you. If you only love the people who love you, you will gain nothing. Even wicked people do that. Be perfect, therefore, as your heavenly Father is perfect."

Jesus taught the people about a humble attitude. "Do not seek attention when you do good acts. When you give to the needy, do not announce it. If you give to the needy, do it in secret. God sees what you do in secret, and he will give you a reward.

"Some people try to pray in public, so that people will notice them. When you pray, go into your room and close the door. There, you can pray to God. God sees what you do in private, and he will reward you.

"When you pray, do not use a lot of words so that people will hear you. That is how the pagans pray. God knows what you need before you ask him for it.

"This is how you should pray: 'Our Father in heaven, hallowed be your name, your kingdom come, your will be done on earth as it is in heaven. Give us today our daily bread. Forgive us our debts, as we also have forgiven our debtors. And lead us not into temptation, but deliver us from the evil one.'

"If you forgive men who sin against you, God will also forgive you. However, if you do not forgive men of their sins, God will not forgive your sins.

"When you fast, do not make faces that show you are hungry. Instead, put oil on your head, and wash yourself. This way, people will not know that you fast. Only God will see what you do, and he will reward you."

Jesus taught the people about what they should value the most. "Do not put your treasures on earth. Objects on earth decay, and thieves steal them. Instead, store treasure in the heaven, where your treasure will never decay and thieves cannot steal it. Your heart will be in the place where you keep your treasure.

"The eye is the lamp of the body. If your eyes are good, then you are full of light. However, if your eyes are bad, you are full of darkness.

"No one can serve two masters. Either he will hate the one and love the other, or he devotes himself to the one and despises the other. In a similar way, it is impossible to serve both God and money."

Jesus taught the people not to worry. "Do not worry about your life, your body, what you will eat or drink, or what you will wear. Life is more important than food, and the body is more important than clothes. The birds of the air do not plant and harvest any food. They do not store things in barns, but God gives them food. Are you not much more valuable than the sparrows? Worry will not add any time to your life.

"In the same way, the lilies do not work, but they look more beautiful than Solomon. God cares for the lilies even though they quickly die. God will care for you even more. Do not wonder what you will eat, drink, or wear. Pagans worry about these things, but God knows that you need them. Instead, seek the Kingdom and God's righteousness, and everything else will come to you as well. Do not worry about tomorrow, because each day has enough worries."

Encourage the children to answer the following questions. There are no right or wrong answers. These questions help the children to understand the story and to apply it to their lives.

1. Is it easy to forgive your enemies? When is it difficult for you to forgive?
2. Do you sometimes feel that it is difficult to pray? What are some methods that will help us pray more effectively?
3. What causes you to worry? How does it feel to allow God to take care of those situations?

Say, **Pretend that you did something nice for a friend. Would you call all of your friends and family and tell them what you did? Sometimes we want a reward when we do something good. However, Jesus told us that we should do good works to honour God--not to honour ourselves. We should do everything in our lives to bring praise and honour to God.**

MEMORY VERSE

Practice the study's memory verse. You will find suggestions for Memory Verse Activities on pages 137-138.

ADDITIONAL ACTIVITIES

Choose from these options to enhance the children's Bible study.

1. Jesus taught us how to pray. As a class, memorize the Lord's Prayer. Think about the meaning of each part of the prayer. How can this prayer teach us to pray more effectively?

2. As a class, think of several needs in your church or your community. Make a list of these items. For each item listed, think of a way that your class could address one of the needs. Select one of these items, and do that activity as a class.

QUESTIONS FOR BASIC COMPETITION

To prepare the children for competition, read Matthew 5:38--6:34 to them.

1 What did Jesus say we should do to an evil person? (5:39)
1. Hit them on the right cheek.
2. **Do not resist them.**
3. Avoid them.

2 What did Jesus say to do to those who persecute us? (5:44)
1. **Pray for them.**
2. Report them to the priest.
3. Persecute them in return.

3 What did Jesus say we should do when we pray? (6:6)
1. Go into your room, and close the door.
2. Pray to your Father, who is unseen.
3. **Both answers are correct.**

4 Why do pagans babble when they pray? (6:7)
1. They like the sound.
2. **They think God will hear them because of their many words.**
3. God answers their prayers more quickly.

5 In the Lord's Prayer, from whom did Jesus ask God for deliverance? (6:13)
1. The Pharisees
2. The Romans
3. **The evil one**

6 Why did Jesus say that people who fast should put oil on their head and wash their face? (6:17-18)
1. Others will see that they love God.
2. **Other people will not know that they fast.**
3. Others will know to stay away from them.

7 Which of these did Jesus say? (6:19)
1. **Do not store up for yourselves some treasures on earth.**
2. Do not store up for yourself some money in the bank.
3. Do not store up for yourself some gold and some silver.

8 Where should we store our treasures? (6:20)
1. On the earth
2. In our house
3. **In the heaven**

9 What two masters did Jesus say we were unable to serve? (6:24)
1. Both God and friends
2. **Both God and money**
3. Both God and family

10 What should we seek first? (6:33)
1. **God's kingdom and righteousness**
2. Money
3. Food and clothing

QUESTIONS FOR ADVANCED COMPETITION

To prepare the children for competition, read Matthew 5:38--6:34 to them.

1 What did Jesus say to do when someone wants to borrow from you? (5:42)
1. Give them everything you have.
2. **Do not turn away from them.**
3. Give them nothing.
4. Give them enough food for their family. Then turn them away.

2 Why are we to love our enemies and pray for our persecutors? (5:44-45)
1. Our Father in heaven will love us.
2. **We may be sons of our Father in heaven.**
3. Our enemies and persecutors will become better people
4. All of the above

3 What must we do when we give to the needy? (6:3)
1. Tell everyone what you give.
2. Give to the needy your old clothing.
3. **Do not let your left hand know what your right hand does.**
4. Announce it so that the people will honour you.

4 Why do hypocrites love to pray in the synagogue and on the street corners? (6:5)
1. **To be seen by men**
2. They are not allowed to pray at home.
3. That is where Jesus told them to pray.
4. All of the above

5 What did Jesus say that people should do when they fast? (6:17)
1. Look sad and put ashes on their faces
2. Stay at home
3. **Put oil on their head and wash their face**
4. Sing praises to God

6 Where did Jesus say your heart would be? (6:21)
1. Where we have family and friends
2. **Where your treasure is**
3. In the heaven
4. On the earth

7 What is more important than food? (6:25)
1. **Our life**
2. Our clothes
3. Our possessions
4. A place to live

8 What does our heavenly Father do for the birds? (6:26)
1. He builds them a nest.
2. **He feeds them.**
3. He helps them fly.
4. He clothes them.

9 What should we do instead of worry? (6:25, 33)
1. Seek peace and joy in little things.
2. Give to the needy.
3. **Seek first God's kingdom and his righteousness.**
4. Seek first to store treasures in heaven.

10 Finish this verse: "Blessed are those who are persecuted because of righteousness . . ." (Matthew 5:10)
1. **". . . for theirs is the kingdom of heaven."**
2. ". . . for they will be comforted."
3. ". . . for God will save them."
4. ". . . for God will punish those who persecute them."

five
Matthew 7:1-29

Memory Verse

"'Blessed are you when people insult you, persecute you and falsely say all kinds of evil against you because of me. Rejoice and be glad because great is your reward in heaven, for in the same way they persecuted the prophets who were before you'" (Matthew 5:11-12).

Biblical Truth

Jesus has authority to teach us how to live because he is the Son of God.

Focus

In this study, children will learn that Jesus taught the people how to live to please God.

Teaching Tip

As you lead the Bible study, you will find many metaphors. A metaphor is a way to describe something by calling it something else. For example, the man is a raging bull. Remember that metaphors can be very difficult for children to understand. Take time to learn about the metaphors mentioned in the Sermon on the Mount and to explain them to your students.

BIBLICAL COMMENTARY

Jesus addressed his followers and gave them advice regarding how to live in relationship with other believers. Jesus wanted his followers to avoid a judgmental attitude toward others. In this passage, Jesus explained that the problem with judging was a self-righteous, hypocritical, condemning attitude. Jesus said that we will be judged in the same way we judge others. If we show others mercy, we will be shown mercy. If we are harsh with others, God will deal harshly with us. We should be careful to discern another person's character truthfully, humbly, and lovingly.

Jesus taught that we must first remove the plank in our own eye. We do that by examining our hearts, minds, and attitudes. Jesus explained that we must address our sins and shortcomings first, so that we may accurately see another person's faults. If we remove the speck from our eye, we can return to our brother and help remove the speck in the eye of the brother. Only after we have experienced the shame and pain of confessing our faults and failures are we fit to evaluate others with humility and compassion. We are then invited, not to condemn, but to help our brothers and sisters in Christ.

CHARACTERISTICS OF GOD

- Jesus has the authority to teach because he is the Son of God.
- God is wise and shares his wisdom with us.

ACTIVITY

You will need these items for this activity:

- Various craft supplies, such as craft sticks, straws, tape, paper clips, etc. Use whatever supplies you have available.
- Two pieces of a fabric that measure the size of a towel
- A timer or a stopwatch

Divide the class into two teams. Give each team an equal amount of supplies. Place the two pieces of fabric on the floor. Have each team build a structure out of their materials on top of the fabric. Tell the teams to build the strongest structure that is possible with the materials. Give each team five minutes to build a structure.

Then, create a "storm" by having you and a helper hold the first piece of fabric by its four corners. Shake the fabric. Use the timer to determine how long it took for the structure to fall apart. Do the same to the other team's structure.

Say, **Even though your buildings seemed strong, the shaky foundation made them fall and collapse. Today you will learn about the strong foundation that we need for our Christian lives.**

BIBLICAL LESSON

Prepare the following story, adapted from Matthew 7:1-29 before you tell it to the children.

Jesus continued with the Sermon on the Mount and said, "Do not judge, or someone will judge you. For in the same way you judge others, you will be judged. Why do you look at the speck of sawdust in your brother's eye and pay no attention to the plank in your eye? First, take the plank out of your eye, and then you will see clearly to remove the speck from the eye of your brother."

"Ask and it will be given to you; seek and you will find; knock and the door will be opened to you. If you know how to give good gifts to your children, your Father in heaven will give even better gifts to those who ask him! So in everything, do to others what you want them to do to you. This sums up the Law and the Prophets."

"Enter through the narrow gate. Many enter through the wide gate and broad road. It leads to destruction. But small is the gate and narrow the road that leads to life, and only a few find it."

"Look out for false prophets. They are like wolves who appear like sheep so they can attack the sheep. Inside, they are mean wolves. You can recognize a false prophet by the result of his prophesies. Every good tree bears good fruit, but a bad tree bears bad fruit. Not everyone who says to me, 'Lord, Lord,' will enter the kingdom of heaven, but only the people who do the will of my Father who is in the heaven. A person who loves God will help other people to love God."

Jesus told the people that they needed a strong faith in God. "Everyone who hears these words of mine and puts them into practice is like a wise man who built his house on the rock. The rain came down, the streams rose, and the winds blew and beat against that house. The house on the rock did not fall, because it had its foundation on the rock. But everyone who hears these words of mine and does not put them into practice is like a foolish man who built his house on the sand. The rain came down, the streams rose, and the winds blew and beat against that house. It fell with a great crash."

When Jesus finished, the people were amazed at what he taught. He taught as one who had authority, and not as their teachers of the Law.

Encourage the children to answer the following questions. There are no right or wrong answers. These questions will help the children to understand the story and to apply it to their lives.

1. **What important ideas did you learn from these verses?**
2. **How are the teachings of Jesus different from the way the people live today?**
3. **What are some examples of attitudes of good fruit and bad fruit? What type of fruit would describe you?**

Say, **Many people listened to Jesus when he was on earth because Jesus was wise. But others listened because they** wanted to learn more about God. Jesus was not just a good man and a wise leader. Some of the things that Jesus taught are not easy for us to hear. Some of the things that Jesus taught are not easy to include in our life. But we believe and obey the teachings of Jesus because he is the Son of God.

MEMORY VERSE

Practice the study's memory verse. You will find suggestions for Memory Verse Activities on pages 137-138.

ADDITIONAL ACTIVITIES

Choose from any of these options to enhance the children's Bible study.

1. Encourage the children to think about times when they have judged others. Spend time in directed prayer, and allow the children an opportunity to ask God for forgiveness for those times. Ask God to reveal to the children the areas of their life that they need to improve.

2. Divide the class into some groups of two students. Ask the children to sit randomly in the room. Say, Imagine that you were in the crowd who heard Jesus as he spoke the Sermon on the Mount. What would you say to a friend about what you saw and heard? Let the children take turns and to tell each other what they saw and heard Jesus say.

QUESTIONS FOR BASIC COMPETITION

To prepare the children for competition, read Matthew 7:1-29 to them.

1 What will happen to those who judge others? (7:1)
1. They will receive punishment.
2. They will die for their sin.
3. **They will be judged.**

2 What did Jesus say to do before you remove the speck from the eye of your brother? (7:5)
1. Remove the plank from the second eye of your brother.
2. **Take the plank out of your eye.**
3. Pay no attention to the plank in your eye.

3 What did Jesus say will happen if people "knock"? (7:7)
1. They will receive an answer.
2. **The door will be opened.**
3. Both answers are correct.

4 What did Jesus say happens when people "seek"? (7:8)
1. **They will find.**
2. They will get lost.
3. They will win the game.

5 What will the Father in the heaven give to those who ask him? (7:11)
1. The answer they need
2. Whatever they want
3. **Good gifts**

6 What did Jesus say that we are to do to others? (7:12)
1. What they have done to us
2. **What we want them to do to us**
3. What Jesus did to people he knew

7 Where do the small gate and narrow road lead? (7:14)
1. To the garden
2. **To life**
3. To your destruction

8 How many people find the road that leads to life? (7:14)
1. **Only a few**
2. Almost everyone
3. No one

9 How can a person recognize a false prophet? (7:16)
1. By their looks
2. **By their fruit**
3. By their clothing

10 What happened to the foolish man's house when the rains came, the streams rose, and the winds blew? (7:27)
1. It floated away.
2. **It fell with a great crash.**
3. It stood firm.

QUESTIONS FOR ADVANCED COMPETITION

To prepare the children for competition, read Matthew 7:1-29 to them.

1 How did Jesus say that the people would be judged? (7:1-2)
   1. **In the same way that they judge others**
   2. The way God wants us to judge them
   3. The way others judge them
   4. The way a jailor judges them

2 What did Jesus say that many people do when they judge others? (7:3-4)
   1. They look at the speck of sawdust in the eye of their brother.
   2. They pay no attention to the plank in their eye.
   3. They say to a brother, "Let me take the speck out of your eye."
   4. **All of the above**

3 How did Jesus say that God's people are to treat others? (7:12)
   1. **"Do to others what you would have them to do to you."**
   2. "Do to others what they did to you."
   3. "Do to others what they did to other people."
   4. "Do good deeds only to good people."

4 Through what type of gate did Jesus tell the people to enter? (7:13-14)
   1. The wide gate
   2. The broad gate on the wide road
   3. **The small gate**
   4. The wide gate on the narrow road

5 How can people recognize a false prophet? (7:15-16)
   1. By their sheep's clothing
   2. **By their fruit**
   3. By their looks--they look like wolves
   4. By their growl

6 What did Jesus say is impossible for a bad tree to do? (7:18)
   1. It cannot bear any fruit in the winter.
   2. It cannot live long.
   3. It cannot produce flowers.
   4. It cannot bear good fruit.

7 Who did Jesus say would enter the kingdom of heaven? (7:21)
   1. Everyone who speaks a prophesy in his name
   2. Everyone who calls him the Lord
   3. **Those who do the will of his Father in the heaven**
   4. Those who drive out demons and perform miracles

8 To whom did Jesus compare people who hear his words and practice them? (7:24)
   1. A prophet who always speaks the truth
   2. **A wise man who built his house on the rock**
   3. A wise man who built his house on the sand
   4. A wise man who could predict the weather

9 Why were the crowds amazed at the teachings of Jesus? (7:28-29)
   1. He told interesting stories.
   2. He quoted the teachers of the Law.
   3. **He taught as one who had authority, and not as their teachers of the Law.**
   4. All of the above.

10 Finish this verse: "Blessed are you when people insult you, persecute you and falsely say all kinds of evil against you because of me..." (Matthew 5:11-12)
   1. **"...Rejoice and be glad, because great is your reward in heaven, for in the same way they persecuted the prophets who were before you."**
   2. "...You will be rewarded greatly because you honour me."
   3. "...I am happy with what you have done, and so is my Father in heaven."
   4. "...Celebrate and be happy, because you have done great things."

SIX
Matthew 8:1-17, 23-34; 9:1-8

Memory Verse

"Your ways, O God, are holy. What god is so great as our God? You are the God who performs miracles; you display your power among the peoples" (Psalm 77:13-14).

Biblical Truth

The miracles of Jesus help us believe that he is the Son of God.

Focus

This lesson will help the children learn that Jesus has power over disease, nature, and evil. He also has the power to forgive sins.

Teaching Tip

As you lead the Bible study, focus on the miracles of Jesus and how they help us to believe that he is the Son of God.

BIBLICAL COMMENTARY

The miracles in this study teach us about the abilities of Jesus. He showed his power over disease and human life when he healed the leper, Peter's mother-in-law, and many others. Jesus showed His power over the supernatural realm when he cast demons from people. He showed His power and authority over the natural world when he calmed the storm on the lake. Jesus has power over all creation. The things that threaten to overpower us cannot defeat Jesus.

These miracles also teach us that Jesus cared for people. When he healed the man who was paralyzed, Jesus revealed that he had the authority to forgive sins. The miracles of Jesus showed that Jesus is the Christ.

Jesus also healed the servant of a Roman centurion. This showed that he also loved people who were not Jews. God offers salvation to all people. He used miracles to demonstrate the love and the compassion of God. The miracles showed that he is the Son of God.

CHARACTERISTICS OF GOD

- Jesus is more powerful than anything that threatens us.
- Jesus has the authority to forgive sins.

WORDS OF OUR FAITH

Faith is trust in God that leads people to believe

45

what God has said, to depend on Him, and to obey Him.

PEOPLE

A **centurion** was a Roman soldier who was in charge of 100 men.

THINGS

Leprosy is a word that describes many different skin diseases.

An **infirmity** was a sickness or handicap.

A **rebuke** is a warning or sharp criticism.

A **miracle** is an amazing event that defies the normal laws of nature. God shows his character and power when he does miracles.

The **Son of Man** is a name for Jesus. This name means that Jesus is God's Son, but he is also human.

ACTIVITY

You will need these items for this activity:

- One mat or one piece of paper for each child in the game
- A sticker or a piece of tape

Before class, place the sticker or the piece of tape on the bottom of one of the pieces of paper or mats. Arrange the mats or pieces of paper in a circle.

Say, **Today, we will stand up from our mats and walk. When I say, "Get up and walk," stand up and move to the left. When I say "Sit," sit down on the nearest mat. If your mat has a piece of tape on** the bottom, you are out of the game!

After a child is out of the game, remove one mat. Take all of the mats up and set them out in a circle in random order. Play until there is only one child left. That child is the winner!

Say, **Jesus did many miracles. Today, we will learn about a man who could not walk. Jesus told him to "get up and walk," and the man walked away! We will also learn about other miracles that Jesus did.**

BIBLICAL LESSON

Prepare the following story, adapted from Matthew 8:1-17, 23-34; 9:1-8, before you tell it to the children.

Large crowds followed Jesus. A man with leprosy came to Jesus, and he said, "Lord, if you are willing, you can make me clean.

Jesus said, "I am willing. Be clean!" Jesus immediately cured the man of his leprosy. Jesus said, "Do not tell anyone what happened to you. Instead, go to the priest, and offer a gift as a testimony to what happened to you."

When Jesus entered Capernaum, a centurion came to him. The centurion said, "Lord, my servant suffers greatly from paralysis."

Jesus said, "I will go and heal him."

The centurion said, "I do not deserve to welcome you into my home. I know that you can heal my servant with a word."

Jesus was surprised by the faith of the

centurion. He said, "I have not met anyone in Israel with faith like this. Go to your servant. He is healed." The servant experienced healing at that exact moment.

Jesus went to the house of Peter. Peter's mother-in-law had a fever. Jesus touched her hand, and her fever disappeared. That evening, many people brought demon-possessed people to Jesus. Jesus drove out the spirits, and he healed many sick people.

Jesus entered into a boat with his disciples. Suddenly, a large storm began on the sea, and large waves splashed over the boat. The disciples said, "Lord, save us! We're going to drown!"

Jesus said, "You of little faith, why are you so afraid?" Jesus rebuked the storm, and the sea became calm.

This miracle amazed the disciples. They said, "What kind of man is this? Even the winds and the waves obey him!"

Jesus arrived in the region of the Gadarenes. Two demon-possessed men lived in the tombs there. They were so violent that no one could approach them. They said to Jesus, "What do you want with us, Son of God? Have you come here to torture us before the appointed time?

There were some pigs nearby. The demons pleaded, "If you drive us out, send us into those pigs."

Jesus said to them, "Go!" The demons came out of the men, and they went into the pigs. The pigs ran down the bank and into the lake. The men who tended the pigs went into the town and told everyone about this. The whole town went to Jesus, and they begged him to leave their region.

Jesus boarded a boat, and he went to his hometown. Some men brought a friend to Jesus. Their friend was paralyzed. Jesus said, "Your sins are forgiven."

Some Jewish scholars said to themselves, "That is blasphemy."

Jesus knew their thoughts. He said, "What is easier to say: 'Your sins are forgiven,' or 'Get up and walk?'" But so that you may know that the Son of Man has authority on earth to forgive sins..." Jesus said to the paralyzed man, "Get up, take your mat, and go home." The man stood up and went home.

When the crowd saw this, they felt amazement, and they praised God.

Encourage the children to answer the following questions. There are no right or wrong answers. These questions help the children to understand the story and to apply it to their lives.

1. Why did the centurion feel that he was not worthy to have Jesus in his house?
2. Why were the disciples afraid of the storm? How does their faith compare to that of the centurion?

Say, **Can you imagine how the people felt about Jesus? Jesus healed the sick with a touch from his hand or a word** from his mouth. They believed in Jesus, and they had faith in his healing power. Jesus is better than a fictional hero. The miracles of Jesus help us to know that our Saviour cares. He also has the power to change lives.

MEMORY VERSE

Practice the study's memory verse. You will find suggestions for Memory Verse Activities on pages 137-138.

ADDITIONAL ACTIVITIES

Choose from these options to enhance the children's Bible study.

1. Make a list of the people in today's study. Compare the faith of each person. What did their faith lead to? What obstacles made faith in God difficult? How did the faith of the disciples compare with the faith of the other people in today's study?

2. Let the children conduct interviews with people who witnessed each of the miracles in this study. Select children to be these persons: interviewer, man who had leprosy, a centurion, Peter's mother-in-law, disciple in the boat who witnessed the calming of the storm, a man cured of his demon-possession. This is not scripted. Let the children review the story as the interviewer asks them to tell about their encounters with Jesus.

QUESTIONS FOR BASIC COMPETITION

To prepare the children for competition, read Matthew 8:1-17, 23-34; 9:1-8 to them.

1 What did a man with leprosy say to Jesus? (8:2)
1. "Stay away from me. I am unclean."
2. **"Lord, if you are willing, you can make me clean."**
3. "Lord, why did this happen to me?"

2 What did Jesus say about the centurion's faith? (8:10)
1. "He did not have enough faith."
2. "No one in the world has faith like this."
3. **"I have not found anyone in Israel with such great faith."**

3 How did Jesus heal Peter's mother-in-law? (8:15)
1. **He touched her hand.**
2. He touched her forehead.
3. He commanded her fever to go away.

4 What happened after Jesus and his disciples got into a boat? (8:23-24)
1. A furious storm came up on the lake.
2. Waves swept over the boat.
3. **Both answers are correct.**

5 From where did two demon-possessed men come to meet Jesus? (8:28)
1. The river
2. **The tombs**
3. The synagogue

6 How did the two demon-possessed men act? (8:28)
1. They screamed day and night.
2. They killed people who came near to them.
3. **They were so violent that no one could pass that way.**

7 What did the people of the town do after Jesus healed the demon-possessed men? (8:34)
1. **They asked him to leave.**
2. They thanked him for his help.
3. They had a feast for Jesus.

8 Who did some men bring to Jesus? (9:1-2)
1. A leper
2. **A paralytic**
3. A demon-possessed man

9 What did Jesus tell the paralytic to do? (9:6)
1. To have great faith
2. To ask to have his sins forgiven
3. **To take up his mat and to go home**

10 What did the crowd do when Jesus healed the paralytic? (9:8)
1. They helped him carry his mat home.
2. **They praised God.**
3. Both answers are correct.

QUESTIONS FOR ADVANCED COMPETITION

To prepare the children for competition, read Matthew 8:1-17, 23-34; 9:1-8 to them.

1 After Jesus healed the leper, what did he tell him to do? (8:3-4)
1. "See that you do not tell anyone."
2. "Go, show yourself to the priest."
3. "Offer the gift that Moses commanded."
4. **All of the above**

2 What happened when Jesus entered Capernaum? (8:5)
1. A leper came to him for healing.
2. **A centurion came to him to ask for help.**
3. A priest came to him to ask a question.
4. A man who was paralyzed came to him.

3 What did Jesus do for Peter's mother-in-law? (8:14-15)
1. He cast a demon out of her.
2. He taught her from the Scriptures.
3. **He healed her fever**.
4. He served to her a meal.

4 What prophecy of Isaiah did Jesus fulfil as He healed the sick and cast out demons? (8:17)
1. **"He took up our infirmities and carried our diseases."**
2. "He loved us, and he gave his life for us."
3. "He healed us by taking our diseases to the Cross."
4. "He proved that he was the Saviour by his healing."

5 What did Jesus say when the disciples woke him during the storm? (8:26)
1. "You of little faith. Do you not know that I can calm storms?"
2. "You were right to wake me."
3. **"You of little faith, why are you so afraid?"**
4. "Great is your faith.'"

6 How did Jesus heal two demon-possessed men who lived in the tombs? (8:28, 32)
1. He prayed for them.
2. **He sent their demons into a herd of pigs.**
3. He cried out, "Demons, come out of them!"
4. All of the above

7 What happened to the herd of pigs? (8:32)
1. They trampled to death the men who tended them.
2. They attacked the two demon-possessed men.
3. They ran into the nearby town.
4. **They rushed down a steep bank into a lake.**

8 What did the teachers of the Law say when Jesus told the paralytic that he forgave his sins? (9:3)
1. **"This fellow is blaspheming!"**
2. "Heal this man first; then forgive his sins."
3. "Who gives you power to forgive sins?"
4. "This man truly needed forgiveness for his sins."

9 Which of these did Jesus tell the paralytic to do? (9:6)
1. To get up
2. To take his mat
3. To go home
4. **All of the above**

10 Finish this verse: "'Your ways, O God, are holy. What god is so great as our God? You are the God who performs miracles; . . .'" (Psalm 77:13-14)
1. "'. . . you are the God above all gods.'"
2. **"'. . . you display your power among the peoples.'"**
3. "'. . . You are the only God who hears our prayers.'"
4. "'. . . You are the only God for us.'"

seven

Matthew 9:9-13, 18-26, 35-38; 10:1-14

Memory Verse

"Then he said to his disciples, 'The harvest is plentiful but the workers are few. Ask the Lord of the harvest, therefore, to send out workers into his harvest field'" (Matthew 9:37-38).

Biblical Truth

Jesus invites us to become his disciples and to join him to build his kingdom.

Focus

This lesson will help children learn that Jesus gave his disciples a message to share and that we should share that same message.

Teaching Tip

As you lead the Bible study, the children may question why Jesus did not want the disciples to go to the Gentiles or to the Samaritans. The message of Jesus was for the Jews first. After Jesus' resurrection, they took the message to all nations.

BIBLICAL COMMENTARY

Tax collectors in the time of Jesus were hated members of society. They were Jews who worked for the Roman oppressors. They became rich at the expense of their neighbours. The Pharisees wanted to know why Jesus would eat with Matthew and his disreputable friends. To eat with someone indicated a relationship. The Pharisees thought Jesus condoned the lifestyles of the tax collectors. In reality, Jesus called Matthew away from his life of sin. The mission of Jesus was to reach out to those who needed him regardless of their status or their reputation.

God wants us to work in his harvest field to bring the people into the covenant community. We pray for more workers. Salvation is not a "God and me" thing. Rather, Jesus wants new believers to join the community that he already established through Israel. We, like Jesus, must reach out to all people with a consistent love.

CHARACTERISTICS OF GOD

- God calls us to follow him and to share his love with others.
- God sends us out to help him to build his kingdom.

WORDS OF OUR FAITH

A disciple is a person who follows the teachings and example of another person. Jesus chose 12

disciples to help him spread the gospel. Today all those who accept and who follow Jesus are his **disciples.**

PEOPLE

The **Zealots** were a group of Jews who believed that only God was the king of Israel. They would fight and die to gain freedom from Rome.

ACTIVITY

You will need these items for this activity:
- Some paper
- Some scissors
- Some pens, pencils, or markers

Before class, Cut out 12 paper fish and write 2-3 words from the memory verse, Matthew 9:37-38, on each fish. Then, hide the fish around the classroom.

Tell the children to find twelve fish that are around the room. Then tell the children to put the fish in correct order. Recite the memory verse together.

BIBLICAL LESSON

Prepare the following story, adapted from Matthew 9:9-13, 18-26, 35-38; 10:1-14 before you tell it to the children.

Jesus saw Matthew who worked as a tax collector. "Follow me," Jesus said to Matthew, and Matthew got up and followed him.

Jesus and his disciples ate dinner at Matthew's house with many tax collectors and sinners. The Pharisees asked the disciples of Jesus, "Why does your teacher eat with tax collectors and sinners?"

Jesus heard what they asked, and he said, "It is not the healthy who need a doctor, but the sick. I have not come to call the righteous. I have come to call the sinners."

While Jesus said this, a ruler came and knelt before him. The ruler told Jesus that his daughter had died that day. He asked Jesus, "Come and put your hand on her, and she will live." So Jesus got up and went with him. His disciples also went with him.

On the way, a woman who had bled for twelve years came behind Jesus, and she touched the edge of his cloak. She said to herself, "If I only touch his cloak, I will be healed." Jesus turned to her, and he said, "Your faith has healed you."

When Jesus entered the ruler's house, he told the crowd to leave. Jesus said, "The girl is not dead. She is asleep." When the crowd went outside, Jesus took the girl by the hand, and she got up.

Jesus went to all the towns and villages. He taught, he preached the good news of the kingdom, and he healed disease and sickness. Jesus had compassion on the people because they were helpless, like sheep without a shepherd. Then Jesus said to his disciples, "The harvest is plentiful but the workers are few."

Jesus gave his disciples the power to

drive out evil spirits and to heal every disease and sickness. There were twelve disciples. Their names were: Simon called Peter and his brother Andrew; James son of Zebedee, his brother John; Philip, Bartholomew, Thomas, Matthew the tax collector, James son of Alphaeus, Thaddaeus, Simon the Zealot, and Judas Iscariot, who betrayed Jesus.

Jesus told his disciples to go to the lost sheep of Israel, not to the Gentiles or to the Samaritans. He told them to preach this message: "The kingdom of heaven is near." He asked the disciples to heal the sick, to raise the dead, to cleanse the lepers, and to drive out demons. Jesus told them that in whatever town or village they entered, they were to search for some worthy person there and stay at his house until they left. Jesus warned that if anyone did not welcome the disciples or listen to their words, they should shake the dust off their feet when they left that home or town.

Encourage the children to answer the following questions. There are no right or wrong answers. These questions will help the children to understand the story and to apply it to their lives.

1. Do you think Matthew and his friends realized what the Pharisees said about them? If so, how do you think they felt?
2. The people made fun of Jesus when He told them the girl was just asleep, not dead. Do you think they believed in Jesus after he raised her to life? Why or why not?
3. Why does God need workers to help him to bring in the harvest?
4. Why would a town reject Jesus and His disciples?

Say, **Do you ever feel like you are not important? Perhaps you feel like you do not have important work to do. This is not true. Jesus calls you to do the most important job in the world—to share the good news about him with people who do not know him. Jesus often looked for ordinary people to help him. Many of these people probably felt very unimportant before they knew Jesus.**

Jesus told them, "The harvest is plentiful but the workers are few" (9:37). Jesus meant that there are a lot of people who do not know about God's love. The people who know Jesus must tell everyone about God's love. Everyone has a job to do for Jesus, and it is an important job.

MEMORY VERSE

Practice the study's memory verse. You will find suggestions for Memory Verse Activities on pages 137-138.

ADDITIONAL ACTIVITIES

Choose from any of these options to enhance the children's Bible study.

1. Who are your closest friends? What makes you so close? Jesus was a role model and mentor to

his disciples. **A mentor is someone who guides you though an activity or series of events or teaches you information. Think about your friends and family. Who is someone who mentors you? What are some things about Jesus you can learn from them? What are some things you can teach them about Jesus?** Encourage the children to make a list of two people in their lives whom they can pray for, disciple, and mentor.

2. Invite a minister to speak to the class about his or her Christian testimony and call to ministry. Give the children time to ask questions. Treat this time with sensitivity. This might be a time when God will call a child in your class into full-time Christian ministry. Let the children know that God asks all Christians to minister to those around them. Some Christians receive a call into a specific full-time ministry.

QUESTIONS FOR BASIC COMPETITION

To prepare the children for competition, read Matthew 9:9-13, 18-26, 35-38; 10:1-14 to them.

1 What did Jesus say to Matthew at the tax collector's booth? (9:9)
   1. "Your sins are forgiven."
   2. **"Follow me."**
   3. "You will be a collector of men."

2 Who ate at Matthew's house with Jesus? (9:10)
   1. Pharisees and teachers of the law
   2. **Many tax collectors and sinners**
   3. Matthew's sick friends

3 What question did the Pharisees ask the disciples of Jesus after they saw Jesus eat at Matthew's house? (9:10-11)
   1. **"Why does your teacher eat with tax collectors and sinners?"**
   2. "Why does your teacher talk to Matthew?"
   3. "Why did Matthew not invite us to dinner?"

4 Which of these did Jesus say to the Pharisees? (9:13)
   1. I desire mercy, not sacrifice.
   2. I have not come to call the righteous, but sinners.
   3. **Both answers are correct**

5 What did the woman who bled for 12 years do? (9:20)
   1. She touched the arm of Jesus.
   2. **She touched the edge of the cloak of Jesus.**
   3. She begged Jesus to heal her.

6 How did Jesus heal the sick daughter of the ruler? (9:25)
   1. **He took her by the hand, and she got up.**
   2. He prayed for her, and she got up.
   3. He touched her forehead, and she got up.

7 What did Jesus do in all of the towns and the villages? (9:35)
   1. He spoke to the teachers of the Law.
   2. He visited his family and his friends.
   3. **He taught, he preached, and he healed.**

8 Why did Jesus have compassion on the crowds? (9:36)
   1. They were sick and needed healing.
   2. **They were helpless, like a sheep without a shepherd.**
   3. They were poor and needy.

9 What did Jesus say to his disciples about the harvest? (9:37)
   1. **The harvest is plentiful, but the workers are few.**
   2. The harvest is poor, and there are too many workers.
   3. The harvest is plentiful. Go and bring it in.

10 What power did Jesus give to his 12 disciples? (10:1)
   1. **He gave the power to drive out evil spirits and to heal every disease and sickness.**
   2. He gave the power to raise the dead.
   3. He gave the power to know the right from the wrong.

QUESTIONS FOR ADVANCED COMPETITION

To prepare the children for competition, read Matthew 9:9-13, 18-26, 35-38; 10:1-14 to them.

1 Who saw Matthew at his tax collector's booth? (9:9)
1. **Jesus**
2. The disciples of Jesus
3. A high priest
4. A Roman ruler

2 What did Jesus say to the Pharisees at Matthew's house? (9:12-13)
1. "It is not the healthy who need a doctor, but the sick."
2. "I desire mercy, not sacrifice."
3. "I have not come to call the righteous, but sinners."
4. **All of the above**

3 Who said, "My daughter has died. But come and put your hand on her, and she will live?" (9:18)
1. A Pharisee
2. **A ruler**
3. A centurion
4. Peter

4 Who went with the ruler whose daughter died? (9:19)
1. **Jesus and his disciples**
2. Only Jesus
3. Jesus and some Pharisees
4. Jesus and a doctor

5 Who touched the edge of the cloak of Jesus as he went to the home of the ruler? (9:19-20)
1. A woman who had a bent back
2. Two children who played
3. A man with a withered arm
4. **A woman who bled for 12 years**

6 What did Jesus say to the flute players and crowd at the house of the ruler? (9:24)
1. "Go away. You cannot help this dead girl."
2. **"Go away. The girl is not dead but asleep."**
3. "Go away. You make too much noise."
4. "Go away. The ruler does not want you here."

7 What instructions did Jesus give to the disciples when he sent them out? (10:5-10)
1. Do not go to the Gentiles or to the Samaritans.
2. Preach that the kingdom of heaven is near.
3. Do not take gold, silver, or copper in your belts.
4. **All of the above**

8 What were the disciples of Jesus to do when they entered a town or a village? (10:11)
1. To search for the synagogue and to begin to teach.
2. To search for the priest and to introduce themselves.
3. **To search for a worthy person with whom they could stay.**
4. To search for an inn where they could stay.

9 What were the disciples to do if someone did not welcome them? (10:14)
1. Pray for the person or the town and leave.
2. Plead with them in the name of Jesus.
3. **Shake the dust off of their feet when they left that person or that town.**
4. Burn down the town.

10 Finish this verse: "Then he said to his disciples, 'The harvest is plentiful but the workers are few. Ask the Lord of the harvest, therefore, . . .'" (Matthew 9:37-38)
1. "'. . . to bring in the harvest soon.'"
2. "'. . . to hire workers for his harvest field.'"
3. **"'. . . to send out workers into his harvest field.'"**
4. "'. . . to help with the hard work.'"

eight

Matthew 11:1-11, 25-30; 12:1-14

Memory Verse

"'Come to me, all you who are weary and burdened, and I will give you rest. Take my yoke upon you and learn from me'" (Matthew 11:28-29a).

Biblical Truth

Jesus reveals the truth about himself and his kingdom to those who seek it.

Focus

This lesson will help children learn that Jesus revealed that he is the Messiah through the good works that he did.

Teaching Tip

As you lead the Bible Study, focus on Jesus' response to John's doubts and the way that God revealed himself through the miracles of Jesus.

BIBLICAL COMMENTARY

The statements and behaviours of Jesus were often unexpected and their meanings were unclear to some. How people responded to the methods of Jesus typically reveal their motives and attitudes toward the things of God.

John the Baptist was the greatest prophet of the Old Covenant era. He prophesied about the Messiah and heard God's voice proclaim that Jesus is his Son. John was a fulfilment of prophecy, and he was obedient to the plan of God for his life. In spite of this, John still had questions about Jesus.

Jesus assured John that Jesus is the Messiah. The evidence of this fact was available for those who were ready to adjust their perspective of the Messiah. Those who believed that Jesus was the Messiah gained a new perspective of God.

The Pharisees were aware also of the messianic signs that Jesus performed. Unlike John, they were not receptive to a deeper understanding of God. The perspective of Jesus on the Sabbath was consistent with the Old Testament. The perspective of the Pharisees on the Sabbath was not. The Pharisees blinded themselves from understanding the Scripture and from understanding correctly the methods of Jesus. The healing of the withered hand should have convinced them of the authority of Jesus. Instead, it made them want to kill him.

CHARACTERISTICS OF GOD

- Jesus proved that he is the Messiah.
- Jesus cares about those who are weary.

WORDS OF OUR FAITH

A **prophet** is someone whom God has chosen to receive and deliver his messages.

THINGS

The **Sabbath** is the day that God set aside to worship him and to rest.

A **yoke** is a wooden bar that connects two animals so that they can work together.

To **humble** oneself is to focus more on God and others than ourselves, and to give praise to God for what he did for us.

ACTIVITY

You will need these items for this activity:

- A chalkboard or a whiteboard
- Twenty-five pieces of paper
- Chalk or dry-erase markers
- Tape

Before class, write the memory verse for the study on the chalkboard or the whiteboard. Use the pieces of paper to cover each word of the memory verse. Number each piece of the paper in numerical order.

Say, **Today we will reveal the memory verse for this study. I will call on someone to tell me a number. I will remove that number from the board. After I remove** the number, we will read the revealed words. Then, the person I call upon will name another member of the class. That person will call out another number.

Continue until the children see every word. Erase the words, and let the students recite the verse as a class.

Say, **We chose the words to reveal in the memory verse for this study. In today's lesson, we will learn how Jesus revealed his true nature through his miracles.**

BIBLICAL LESSON

Prepare the following story, adapted from Matthew 11:1-11, 25-30; 12:1-14, before you tell it to the children.

Jesus taught his disciples many things about how God wants the followers of Jesus to live. Jesus and his disciples went to Galilee to teach and to preach.

John the Baptist heard that Jesus was nearby. John sent his disciples to ask Jesus, "Are you the one who was to come, or should we expect someone else?"

Jesus said, "Go back to John. Tell him that the blind now see. The lame now walk, and people with leprosy are healthy. The deaf now hear, and the dead are now alive."

When the disciples of John left, Jesus spoke to the crowd. He said, "Did you come into the desert to see a reed swayed by the wind? If not, what did you want to see? Did you want to see a man who wears nice clothes? No, because a man

with nice clothes lives in a palace. Did you come to see a prophet? Yes, you did. You saw someone who is more than a prophet. This person is John the Baptist, and no one rose higher than he has. In spite of this, the lowest person in the kingdom of heaven will be higher than John."

Jesus spoke about his relationship to God, the Father. He said, "I praise you, Father. You are the Lord of everything. You revealed your nature to little children.

"You have entrusted me with many things, Father. No one knows the Son except the Father, and no one knows the Father except the Son and those to whom the Son chooses to reveal him."

Jesus knew the people were sometimes weary. He said, "If you are weary, come to me and I will give you rest. Take my yoke upon you and learn from me. I am gentle and humble. I will give you rest, because my yoke is easy and my burden is light."

The Jewish leaders had many rules about the Sabbath. On the Sabbath, Jesus went through some grain fields with his disciples. When the disciples became hungry, they picked heads of grain and ate them. The Pharisees saw this. They said, "Your disciples do not honour the Sabbath. They do what is unlawful."

Jesus said "When David and his men were hungry, they ate the bread in the tabernacle. In a similar way, the Scripture says that the priests desecrate the Sabbath. However, they are innocent. Some-one is here who is greater than the temple. The Son of Man is Lord of the Sabbath."

Jesus went into the synagogue where he met a man with a shrivelled hand. The Pharisees wanted a reason to accuse Jesus, so they asked, "Is it lawful to heal on the Sabbath?"

Jesus said, "If your sheep falls into a pit on the Sabbath, you will lift it out. A man is much more valuable than a sheep. Therefore, it is lawful to do good on the Sabbath."

Jesus said to the man, "Stretch out your hand." The man stretched out his hand, and it was healthy. This made the Pharisees angry, and they plotted a way to kill Jesus.

Encourage the children to answer the following questions. There are no right or wrong answers. These questions help the children to understand the story and to apply it to their lives.

1. Why did John want to know if Jesus is the Messiah? Have you ever asked God to help you know or understand something? What was it?

2. Jesus showed that he is the Messiah when he performed miracles. What are some other ways that Jesus showed he is the Messiah?

3. Jesus confronted the Pharisees in Matthew 12:1-14. How do you think the Pharisees felt? Has someone ever confronted you? How did you feel?

Say, **Are there times in your life when you are confused? Often, people become confused about who God is. They may feel confusion about how God wants them to live. In the same way that John allowed Jesus to remove his confusion about who Jesus is, Jesus can help us with our confusion. When we read the Bible, pray, and accept Jesus as the Son of God, we can gain a truer perspective of who God is. We can also gain a clearer understanding of how we should live.**

MEMORY VERSE

Practice the study's memory verse. You will find suggestions for Memory Verse Activities on pages 137-138.

ADDITIONAL ACTIVITIES

Choose from these options to enhance the children's Bible study.

1. While John was in prison, he received encouragement from Jesus. As a class, think of ways that you can encourage people. Write messages to two people in your church or community to encourage them.

2. Discuss whether God performs miracles today. Ask the children to interview some adults and find out if the adults are aware of any miracles God has performed. Let the children report about what they learn.

QUESTIONS FOR BASIC COMPETITION

To prepare the children for competition, read Matthew 11:1-11, 25-30; 12:1-14 to them.

1 Who heard in prison what Christ did? (11:2)
   1. Peter and James
   2. James and John
   3. John the Baptist

2 What did John the Baptist do when he heard what Jesus did? (11:2-3)
   1. He sent his disciples to talk to Jesus.
   2. He escaped from jail to see Jesus.
   3. He praised God for all that Jesus did.

3 What question did the disciples of John ask Jesus? (11:3)
   1. "When will you die on the Cross for us?"
   2. "Are you the one who was to come, or should we expect someone else?"
   3. Both answers are correct.

4 According to Jesus, what Old Testament prophecy talks about John the Baptist? (11:10)
   1. "I will make him a great prophet."
   2. "I will send my messenger ahead of you."
   3. "Someday he will wear fine clothes."

5 What invitation did Jesus give to the people? (11:28)
   1. "Come to me all of you who are poor, and I will supply your needs."
   2. "Come to me, all of you who are hungry, and I will feed you."
   3. "Come to me, all you who are weary and burdened, and I will give you rest."

6 What did Jesus say about his yoke and his burden? (11:30)
   1. "My yoke is easy and my burden is light."
   2. "My yoke and my burden fit everyone perfectly."
   3. "My yoke and my burden make you strong."

7 What did the hungry disciples of Jesus do during one Sabbath? (12:1)
   1. They picked the heads of the grain, and they ate them.
   2. They turned the stones into bread.
   3. They went to the lake to fish.

8 Who did Jesus say is Lord of the Sabbath? (12:8)
   1. God the Father
   2. The angels in heaven
   3. The Son of Man

9 When Jesus went to a synagogue, what special person was there? (12:9-10)
   1. The high priest from Jerusalem
   2. A man with a shrivelled hand
   3. A woman who was blind for 12 years

10 How did Jesus answer the question of the Pharisees about healing on the Sabbath? (12:10,12)
   1. "I never heal on the Sabbath."
   2. "Sometimes it is right to heal on the Sabbath."
   3. "It is lawful to do good on the Sabbath."

QUESTIONS FOR ADVANCED COMPETITION

To prepare the children for competition, read Matthew 11:1-11, 25-30; 12:1-14 to them.

1 Where was John the Baptist when he heard what Christ did? (11:2)
1. **Prison**
2. The court of Herod
3. The desert
4. The home of his parents

2 Which of these did Jesus tell the disciples of John to report to him? (11:4-5)
1. "The blind receive sight."
2. "Those who have leprosy are cured."
3. "The dead are raised, and the good news is preached to the poor."
4. **All of the above**

3 How did Jesus describe John the Baptist? (11:11)
1. "He is the best friend that anyone could want."
2. **"Among those born of women there has not risen anyone greater than John the Baptist."**
3. "I am a prophet, but John is more than a prophet."
4. All of the above

4 Which of these did Jesus invite people to do? (11:29)
1. To tell some parables
2. **To take his yoke and learn from him**
3. To ride a donkey
4. All of the above

5 Who picked and ate heads of grain on the Sabbath? (12:1)
1. Jesus and his disciples
2. Jesus and a crowd of people
3. **The disciples of Jesus**
4. The disciples and their wives

6 What did the Pharisees say to Jesus when his disciples picked and ate grain on the Sabbath? (12:2)
1. **"Your disciples are doing what is unlawful on the Sabbath."**
2. "Your disciples are very wise."
3. "Your disciples have broken the laws of our nation."
4. "Your disciples should not eat so much."

7 What did Jesus say when the Pharisees said that the disciples broke the Sabbath? (12:3-8)
1. "David ate the consecrated bread that only the priests were to eat."
2. "Priests desecrate the Sabbath, but they are innocent."
3. "Someone greater than the temple is here."
4. **All of the above**

8 What did Jesus do for the man with the shrivelled hand? (12:13)
1. **He restored it when the man stretched out his hand.**
2. He stretched the hand to the proper length.
3. He prayed for the man, and he healed his hand.
4. He refused to do anything because it was the Sabbath.

9 After Jesus healed the man with the withered hand, what did the Pharisees do? (12:14)
1. They praised God.
2. They thanked Jesus for this miracle.
3. **They plotted how to kill Jesus.**
4. They angrily rebuked Jesus.

10 Finish this verse: "Come to me, all you who are weary and burdened..." (11:28-29*a*)
1. "...and I will give you peace. Learn from my teachings."
2. "...and I will give you rest. Come whenever you need rest."
3. "...and you will find rest for your souls."
4. **"...and I will give you rest. Take my yoke upon you and learn from me."**

nine

Matthew 13:1-23, 31-35, 44-46, 53-58

Memory Verse

"'But seek first his kingdom and his righteousness, and all these things will be given to you as well'" (Matthew 6:33).

Biblical Truth

God wants us to understand his kingdom, and Jesus used parables to teach these truths.

Focus

In this lesson, children will learn that Jesus compared the kingdom of heaven to many things so that we might better understand it.

Teaching Tip

As you lead the Bible study, help the children to understand the difference between the different types of soil. As a class, come up with examples of how a person from each category might live and act.

BIBLICAL COMMENTARY

The disciples asked Jesus why he taught in parables. Parables were good illustrations of the kingdom. But, some people did not understand their meaning. Some of the people who heard Jesus were stubborn troublemakers who found fault in everyone. They heard his words and saw his miracles, but they truly did not hear or see who Jesus really is.

The disciples often did not understand the parables. However, unlike those who were spiritually blind and deaf, the disciples paid attention, and they asked what the parables meant. The disciples really cared about Jesus, and they wanted to obey him. The disciples wanted to learn about God and to understand Jesus better.

Jesus wants us to search diligently to understand who he is. He wants us to obey him. He wants everyone to be a part of the kingdom of God.

CHARACTERISTICS OF GOD

- God gives us the Bible to help us understand how we can obey him.

WORDS OF OUR FAITH

A **parable** is a story that uses familiar items to teach a special lesson. Jesus used **parables** to explain ideas about God or his kingdom.

ACTIVITY

You will need these items for this activity:

- Pieces of paper (twice as many as the number of children in your class)
- A pen, a pencil, or a marker

Before class, write some items that children consider valuable on some pieces of paper. Include some items such as food, shelter, God, and family. Fold the pieces of paper in half.

During class, instruct the children to sit in a circle, and ask each child to choose a piece of paper. Each child can choose to keep his or her piece of paper or trade it possibly to receive a piece of paper with something potentially more valuable on it. Let the children open the papers and read the words on them. Discuss the value of each item or each person.

Say, **For what would you spend all of your money? What would you do with that item to keep it safe?**

Read Matthew 13:44-46 to the children. Say, **What did the people in the story do with their valuable items? What do you think Jesus meant when he compared these items to the kingdom of heaven?** (The kingdom of heaven is so valuable that we should give up everything to receive it.)

BIBLICAL LESSON

Prepare the following story, adapted from Matthew 13:1-23, 31-35, 44-46, 53-58 before you tell it to the children.

Jesus sat by the lake as he talked to the people. Large crowds gathered around him on the shore, so he stepped into a boat and sat in it to teach. He told the people many things in parables. A parable is a story that uses familiar items to teach a spiritual lesson.

Jesus said, "A farmer went out to sow his seed. Some seed fell along the path, and the birds came and ate the seed. Some seed fell on rocky places, where it did not have much soil. The plants withered because the soil was shallow. Other seed fell among thorns that grew up and "choked the plants." Other seed fell on good soil, where it produced a crop--a hundred, sixty or thirty times more than the seed." Then Jesus said, "He who has ears, let him hear."

The disciples asked Jesus why he spoke to the people in parables. Jesus said, "They hear but they do not understand. The hearts of the people have become hard." Jesus told the disciples that they receive blessings because they see, hear, and understand.

Then Jesus explained the parable of the sower. When anyone hears the message about the kingdom but does not understand it, the evil one comes along and steals away the message. This is like the seed sown along the path. The seed that fell on rocky places is like the person who hears the word and receives it with joy. However, like a plant with no root, when

trouble comes along, he quickly gives up. The seed that fell among the thorns is like the person who hears the word, but the worries of life choke the message and make it unfruitful. But, the person who receives the word, understands it, and allows it to grow and make a difference is like the seed that fell on good soil.

Then Jesus told the people another parable. He said, "The kingdom of heaven is like a mustard seed that a man planted in his field. It is a small seed, but it grows into a large tree in which the birds can sit in its branches.

The kingdom of heaven is also like yeast that is worked all through the dough and makes the dough rise.

Jesus told the crowd all of these things in parables. He did not say anything to them without using a parable.

Jesus said, "The kingdom of heaven is like a treasure that someone hid in a field. When a man found it, he hid it again. Then, in his joy, he sold all that he owned, and he bought that field. The kingdom of heaven is like a merchant who looks for fine pearls. When he found one of great value, he went away and sold everything that he owned, and he bought it."

After Jesus finished these parables, he went to his hometown to teach the people. The people felt amazement at his wisdom and his power. However, they thought of him only as the son of Mary and Joseph. Jesus said, "Only in his hometown and in his own house is a prophet without honour." Jesus did not do many miracles there because of their lack of faith.

Encourage the children to answer the following questions. There are no right or wrong answers. These questions will help the children to understand the story and to apply it to their lives.

1. How does the Parable of the Sower relate to your life and the way you react to God? Which type of soil are you?

2. How does the kingdom of heaven relate to a mustard seed and yeast?

3. Why was Jesus not accepted in his town? Do you think this happens to ministers or other people today? Share any examples you have.

Say, **Jesus used parables to teach the people about his kingdom. Parables used examples and items that were familiar to the people. In order for the people to understand the deeper meaning, their minds must receive the lesson that Jesus taught them.**

God's Word will spread throughout the world. Everyone will make the choice to believe or not to believe. Jesus wants us to choose to follow him. What choice have you made?

MEMORY VERSE

Practice the study's memory verse. You will find suggestions for Memory Verse Activities on pages 137-138

ADDITIONAL ACTIVITIES

Choose from any of these options to enhance the children's Bible study.

1. As a class, plant some beans or grass seeds. As you plant the seeds, ask these questions: **What does a plant need to grow? Why did Jesus compare the kingdom of heaven to seeds that fell among different kinds of soil?** As a class, care for the seeds until they sprout and form a plant. After the plant has grown, encourage the children to show the plant to someone and tell the person the parable of the seeds.

2. Research the importance of a mustard seed. Ask, **How much can you reap from a mustard seed plant? Why did Jesus compare the kingdom of heaven to a mustard seed?** Also research the importance of yeast. Try to follow a yeast bread recipe twice, once with yeast, once without yeast. Ask, **What is the difference and similarity between the two batches of bread? Why did Jesus compare the kingdom of heaven to yeast?**

QUESTIONS FOR BASIC COMPETITION

To prepare the children for competition, read Matthew 13:1-23, 31-35, 44-46, 53-58 to them.

1 Who went out to sow his seed? (13:3)
1. A farmer's wife
2. A farmer
3. A farmer and his son

2 What happened to the seed that fell along the path? (13:4)
1. People walked on it.
2. Birds ate it.
3. Both answers are correct.

3 What happened to the seed that fell among the thorns? (13:7)
1. The thorns ate the plants.
2. The thorns and seeds grew well together.
3. The thorns choked the plants.

4 What happened to the seed that fell on good soil? (13:8)
1. It produced a crop--two times more than the seed.
2. It produced a crop--a hundred, sixty, or thirty times more than the seed.
3. It produced a crop--300 times more than the seed.

5 Why did Jesus say that he taught the people in the parables? (13:15)
1. They did not understand real stories.
2. They liked the parables.
3. Their hearts were calloused.

6 The seed that fell on good soil produced more seed. Who does this describe? (13:8, 23)
1. The person who hears the Word of God and understands it.
2. The person who uses magical powers.
3. Both answers are correct.

7 What happens to a mustard seed when you plant it? (13:32)
1. It withers and dies because it has no root.
2. It grows into a small plant.
3. It grows into a big tree where birds can sit in the branches.

8 When a man found hidden treasure in a field, what did he do? (13:44)
1. He hid the treasure again.
2. He sold everything that he owned, and he bought the field where the treasure was.
3. Both answers are correct.

9 When Jesus went to his hometown, what did he do? (13:54)
1. He taught the people in the synagogue.
2. He sold all his possessions and gave the money to the synagogue.
3. He argued with the priest in the synagogue.

10 How did people in his hometown feel about what Jesus taught? (13:54, 57)
1. They were amazed.
2. They were upset at him.
3. Both answers are correct.

QUESTIONS FOR ADVANCED COMPETITION

To prepare the children for competition, read Matthew 13:1-23, 31-35, 44-46, 53-58 to them.

1 Jesus used stories to teach the people. What kind of stories did Jesus use? (13:3)
   1. **Some parables**
   2. Fairy tales
   3. History lessons
   4. Real stories about the disciples

2 What kind of seed sprang up quickly, because the soil was shallow? (13:5)
   1. **The seed that fell on rocky places**
   2. The seed that fell on good soil
   3. The seed that fell along the path
   4. The seed that fell among the thorns

3 What is the seed that fell on thorny soil like? (13:22)
   1. **Someone who hears the word, but the deceitfulness of wealth and worries of life make it unfruitful**
   2. Someone who is so lazy that he does not pull the weeds from his field
   3. Someone who does not have enough money to care for his field properly
   4. All of the above

4 Who does the seed that fell on good soil represent? (13:23)
   1. Those who live good lives and do many good deeds
   2. Those who are 100, 60, or 30 times better than other people
   3. Those whose goodness is equal to the goodness of God.
   4. **Those who hear the Word of God, understand it, and produce a great crop for God**

5 To what did Jesus compare the kingdom of heaven? (13:31, 33)
   1. A mustard seed and a wheat seed
   2. **A mustard seed and yeast**
   3. Flour and yeast
   4. Salt and pepper

6 What did the man who found the hidden treasure do? (13:44)
   1. **He hid it again, sold all that he owned, and bought the field where the treasure was.**
   2. He dug it up, and he took it.
   3. He bought the treasure from the man who owned the field.
   4. He left it in the field because it was not his.

7 How did the crowd react when Jesus taught in his hometown? (13:54, 57)
   1. They were amazed and asked him to speak again.
   2. **They were both amazed and offended.**
   3. They were offended, and they tried to kill him.
   4. They called him a "prophet without honour."

8 What did the people in the hometown of Jesus say about him? (13:55-56)
   1. Is not this the son of the carpenter?
   2. Are not his brothers James, Joseph, Simon, and Judas?
   3. Where then did this man get all of these things?
   4. **All of the above**

9 Why did not Jesus do many miracles in his hometown? (13:58)
   1. **The people lacked faith.**
   2. The people did not want any miracles.
   3. The people trusted in God, but they did not trust in Jesus.
   4. There was no time to do miracles.

10 Finish this verse: "But seek first his kingdom and his righteousness, . . ." (Matthew 6:33)
   1. ". . . and God will answer all of your prayers."
   2. ". . . and you will become a very righteous person."
   3. **". . . and all these things will be given to you as well."**
   4. ". . . and you will live long in the land the Lord, your God promised you."

ten Matthew 14:1-36

Memory Verse

"Cast your cares on the Lord and he will sustain you; he will never let the righteous fall" (Psalm 55:22).

Biblical Truth

Because Jesus cares for us, we can trust him.

Focus

This lesson will help the children learn that Jesus cares for us. Because of this, he is worthy of our trust.

Teaching Tip

As you lead the Bible study, focus on the way that the miracles of Jesus display his care for people. Jesus took care of people despite his own exhaustion and his need to be alone.

BIBLICAL COMMENTARY

When Jesus heard of John the Baptist's death, he withdrew to a "solitary place." Jesus probably wanted to spend time with God in prayer and to mourn for John. However, when Jesus arrived at this place, he found a crowd waiting for him. Jesus felt compassion for them.

Jesus told the disciples to feed the people. The disciples did not have enough food for everyone. They presented their meagre resources to Jesus in obedience to his command. Jesus praised God for providing the loaves and fish, and he broke them into pieces. Jesus returned the pieces to the disciples, who served the food to the crowd. There was enough food for everyone, with an abundance left over.

CHARACTERISTICS OF GOD

- Jesus cares for us, and he is able to supply our needs.
- Jesus is worthy of our trust.

WORDS OF OUR FAITH

King Herod was Herod Antipas. He was the half-brother of King Philip.

John the Baptist was a man who prepared the way for Jesus. He preached about the need to repent.

A **tetrarch** was a person who ruled one quarter of a kingdom or land.

Herodias was King Philip's former wife. She married Herod Antipas.

PLACES

Gennesaret was a narrow plain about six and a half kilometres long and three kilometres wide (about four miles long and two miles wide) on the northwest coast of the Sea of Galilee.

THINGS

An **oath** is a promise.

A **solitary place** is a place where someone goes to be alone.

The **fourth watch** were the hours between 3 AM and 6 AM

ACTIVITY

You will need these items for this activity:
- A small chair
- A blindfold
- Two adult volunteers

Before the class, explain the rules to the adult volunteers. The adult volunteers will hold a chair between them. Keep the chair about 15 centimetres off of the ground. A student volunteer with a blindfold will sit in the chair and place his or her hands on the shoulders of the adults. The adults will then pretend to raise the chair into the air. The adults will keep the chair in the same place, but move into a position on their knees. The student volunteer will feel like he or she is high in the air.

Say, **When Jesus walked on the water, he invited Peter to follow him. Peter did not know what would happen, but he fol-** lowed Jesus. Now you will take a step of faith! Move off of the chair, and step onto the ground! Be prepared to catch the child in case he or she stumbles.

Say, **Peter became afraid when he saw the waves around him. He forgot that Jesus would care for him. Today we will learn how Jesus cares for all of us.**

BIBLICAL LESSON

Prepare the following story, adapted from Matthew 14:1-36, before you tell it to the children.

King Herod heard of the miraculous things that Jesus did. He said, "This man is John the Baptist. He returned from the dead."

King Herod said this because earlier he arrested John and put him in prison. Herod imprisoned John to please Herodias, the wife of Herod's brother, Philip. Herodias did not like John because John said to Philip, "It is not lawful for you to have Herodias as your wife." Herod wanted to kill John, but he was afraid of the people. The people believed that John was a prophet.

On Herod's birthday, the daughter of Herodias danced for Herod. Herod was pleased, and he promised to give her anything that she wanted. Herodias told her daughter to ask for the head of John the Baptist on a platter. The request worried Herod, but he kept his promise. He ordered his men to behead John. An official

brought the head of John to Herodias and her daughter. The disciples of John buried his body, and then they told Jesus what happened.

When Jesus heard what happened to John, he went to a solitary place. The crowds heard that Jesus went to this place, and they followed him there. Jesus saw the large crowd, and he healed their sick.

The disciples came to Jesus as evening approached. They said, "It is late, and this place is remote. Send the crowds away so that they can buy food for themselves."

Jesus said, "They do not need to go away. You give them something to eat."

The disciples said, "We only have five loaves of bread and two fish."

Jesus said, "Bring them to me." Jesus told the people to sit. Jesus gave thanks to God for the bread and the fish, and he broke them into pieces. Then, Jesus told the disciples to pass the food to the people in the crowd. All of the people ate as much as they wanted. The disciples picked up the food that was left, and it filled twelve baskets. In total, the food fed five thousand men, along with women and children.

Jesus sent his disciples ahead of him on a boat. He dismissed the crowd, and then he went up the mountain to pray. The boat was a large distance from land, and the wind became very strong. The waves and the wind buffeted the boat.

Early in the morning, Jesus walked on the water to come to the disciples. The disciples believed that Jesus was a ghost, and they were afraid. Jesus said, "Do not be afraid. It is I."

Peter said, "Lord, if it is you, tell me to come to you on the water."

Jesus said, "Come."

Peter went out to Jesus. However, when he saw the wind and the waves, he was afraid, and he began to sink. Peter said, "Lord, save me!"

Immediately, Jesus reached out and caught Peter. Jesus said to Peter, "You of little faith, why did you doubt?"

When Jesus and Peter climbed into the boat, the wind and waves calmed. The disciples said, "Truly you are the Son of God."

When Jesus and the disciples reached the other side of the lake, they landed at Gennesaret. The men of Gennesaret recognized Jesus, and they sent word to other people. People brought their sick to Jesus, and everyone who touched him became well.

Encourage the children to answer the following questions. There are no right or wrong answers. These questions help the children to understand the story and to apply it to their lives.

1. How do you think Jesus felt when he heard that John was dead? Has someone you loved died? Why did Jesus need to pray afterwards?

2. Jesus fed a large crowd of people with only five loaves of bread and

two fish. How do you think the crowd felt when they witnessed this miracle? Have you ever seen something miraculous? How did you feel?

3. Why did Jesus invite Peter to follow him onto the water? Have you felt that God asked you to do something difficult? How did you feel about it?

Say, **How do you know if someone cares about you or loves you? How do people show their love and their concern for others? People show they care for others when they share with them. They also show they care when they spend time with them. In our lesson today, Jesus showed that he cared by his deeds of compassion. He healed the sick, and he fed those who were hungry.**

In the midst of the stresses of life, Jesus comes to us with his love and compassion. Jesus reaches out to us, just as he reached out to Peter. Jesus cares about each of us, and he wants the best for our lives. He wants us to trust him.

MEMORY VERSE

Practice the study's memory verse. You will find suggestions for Memory Verse Activities on pages 137-138.

ADDITIONAL ACTIVITIES

Choose from any of these options to enhance the children's Bible study.

1. As a class, research the Sea of Galilee. How was it important during the time of Jesus? How is it important today?

2. Peter followed Jesus out onto the water. As a class, look for other instances that show this impetuous side of Peter. Some suggested passages are Matthew 16:13-20; 26:31-35, 50-51; and John 13:6-8. How did Peter's time with Jesus change Peter?

QUESTIONS FOR BASIC COMPETITION

To prepare the children for competition, read Matthew 14:1-36 to them.

1 What did Herod do to John the Baptist? (14:1, 3)
1. He arrested him, and he beat him.
2. He argued with him about Herodias.
3. **He arrested him, and he put him in prison.**

2 What did Herodias's daughter do for Herod on his birthday? (14:6)
1. She sang to him.
2. **She danced for him.**
3. She cooked for him.

3 Why did Herod agree to give to the daughter of Herodias the head of John the Baptist on a platter? (14:9)
1. **Because of his oaths and his dinner guests**
2. Because he was glad to get rid of John
3. Because he loved the daughter of Herodias

4 What happened when Jesus saw the large crowd that followed him to a solitary place? (14:14)
1. He had compassion on them.
2. He healed their sick.
3. **Both answers are correct.**

5 When evening came, what did the disciples of Jesus tell him to do? (14:15)
1. **"Send the crowd away to buy food."**
2. "Feed the crowd with five loaves and two fish."
3. Both answers are correct.

6 What did Jesus do before he broke the five loaves? (14:19)
1. He showed the loaves to the crowd.
2. **He looked up to heaven, and he gave thanks.**
3. Both answers are correct.

7 How many people ate the five loaves and two fish? (14:21)
1. 5,000 people
2. **5,000 men plus women and children**
3. The disciples of Jesus and some women and some children

8 When Jesus walked on water, what did Peter ask Jesus to do? (14:28)
1. "Show me how to walk on water."
2. "Get into the boat and save us."
3. **"Tell me to come to you on the water."**

9 When Peter saw the wind, what happened? (14:30)
1. **He was afraid, and he began to sink.**
2. He tried to fly through the wind.
3. He raised his hands.

10 When Jesus arrived in Gennesaret, what did people do? (14:35-36)
1. They brought their sick and left them with Jesus.
2. **They begged Jesus to let their sick people touch the edge of his cloak.**
3. Both answers are correct.

QUESTIONS FOR ADVANCED COMPETITION

To prepare the children for competition, read Matthew 14:1-36 to them.

1 Why did Herod not kill John the Baptist when he first wanted to do that? (14:5)
1. **He was afraid of the people, who thought John was a prophet.**
2. He wanted a chance to talk to John.
3. He wanted to wait for a good opportunity.
4. He secretly liked the preaching of John.

2 For what did the daughter of Herodias ask from Herod? (14:8)
1. To be Herod's queen
2. To marry John the Baptist
3. For gold and jewels for herself
4. **For the head of John the Baptist on a platter**

3 To whom did the daughter of Herodias carry the head of John the Baptist? (14:11)
1. Herod
2. The disciples of John
3. **Her mother**
4. Jesus

4 How much food did the disciples have? (14:17)
1. **Five loaves of bread and two fish**
2. Two loaves of bread and five fish
3. Four loaves of bread and three fish
4. Seven loaves of bread and three fish

5 What did Jesus do before he broke the loaves? (14:19)
1. He told the people to sit on the grass.
2. He looked up to heaven.
3. He gave thanks.
4. **All of the above**

6 After Jesus fed the 5,000, what did He do? (14:23)
1. He got into a boat to go to the other side of a lake.
2. He went further into the desert to pray.
3. **He went up a mountain by himself to pray.**
4. He went into the nearest town to sleep.

7 What did Jesus say to his frightened disciples who saw him walk on water? (14:27)
1. **"Take courage! It is I. Don't be afraid."**
2. "Don't be afraid. Come out on the water to me."
3. "Take courage! These winds will die down soon."
4. All of the above

8 Why did Peter begin to sink when he went to Jesus on the water? (14:30)
1. He saw a ghost.
2. **He saw the wind, and he was afraid.**
3. The disciples cried out to him.
4. He did not see Jesus.

9 What did the people of Gennesaret do when Jesus landed there? (14:34-35)
1. They recognized Jesus.
2. They sent word to the surrounding country.
3. They brought their sick to Jesus.
4. **All of the above**

10 Finish this verse: "Cast your cares on the LORD..." (Psalm 55:22)
1. "...and he will uphold you; he will never let the righteous lack for anything."
2. **"...and he will sustain you; he will never let the righteous fall."**
3. "...and he will deliver you; he will never let the faithful fall in battle."
4. "...and he will answer you; you are more precious to him than gold."

eleven

Matthew 15:21-28; 16:13-28; 17:1-9

Memory Verse

"Simon Peter answered, 'You are the Christ, the Son of the living God'" (Matthew 16:16).

Biblical Truth

Jesus blesses those who believe he is the Son of God.

Focus

In this lesson, children will learn that Jesus is truly the Son of God.

Teaching Tip

Take time to research this study's passages to be sure you understand them. These scriptures are difficult for children to understand. Yet they are very important passages to help everyone understand the divinity of Jesus.

BIBLICAL COMMENTARY

This lesson focuses on the identity of Jesus as the Son of God. In the first passage, a woman called Jesus the Son of David--a title for the promised Messiah. This passage confuses some people. Jesus referred to the Gentiles when he spoke of the dogs and of the Jews when he spoke of the children. The statement of Jesus means, "It is not right to share the gospel with non-Jews before I teach it to the Jews." Though the woman was a Gentile, she had her faith in Jesus. She understood who he was better than many of the Jews. Because of this faith, Jesus blessed her with a miracle.

In the second passage, Jesus asked his disciples to tell him who the people thought that Jesus was. Many people said that Jesus was a prophet. However, Peter said that Jesus was the Messiah, and the "Son of the living God". This deeper understanding of the identity of Jesus brought a blessing and prepared the disciples to hear more about the mission of Jesus.

Finally, the Transfiguration gave greater evidence of the divinity of Jesus. The appearance of Jesus changed. Jesus was in a glorified state.

CHARACTERISTICS OF GOD

- Jesus is the Christ.
- Jesus is God's Son.

WORDS OF OUR FAITH

To **Confess** is to admit or acknowledge something. For example, you admit to God that you have done wrong. Or, you acknowledge that Christ is the Lord.

Christ comes from the Greek, *christos,* meaning "anointed one" and is similar in meaning to the Hebrew Messiah.

PEOPLE

Son of David is another name for Jesus. This name is a title that the Jews gave to the Messiah.

Jeremiah was a prophet who warned the people of Judah to repent and to turn to God.

Elijah was a famous prophet of Israel.

PLACES

Caesarea Philippi was a city north of the Sea of Galilee near Mt. Hermon.

Mt. Hermon was the place where the transfiguration of Jesus probably happened. It was about 16 kilometers north of Caesarea Philippi.

OTHER TERMS

To **"deny self"** is a commitment not to live selfishly.

To **"take up your cross"** is a strong commitment to follow Jesus, even to the point of death.

The **Transfiguration** is the event where three disciples saw Jesus in his glorification. The appearance of Jesus changed and his face shone. From within a cloud, God told to the disciples that Jesus is his Son.

ACTIVITY

You will need these items for this activity:

• A soft ball

Instruct the children to stand in a circle. The teacher will say, "I am (teacher's name). Who do you say that I am?" The teacher will then toss the ball to a child across the circle from him or her. The child who catches the ball must respond with who he or she says the teacher is. For example, the child might say, "You are my teacher." Then the child repeats the question by saying, "I am (child's name). Who do you say that I am?" The child will toss the ball to another child in the circle who will respond with who he or she says that the child is. Play this game until every child has an opportunity to speak.

Say, **In today's lesson, we will hear the question, "Who do you say that I am?" asked by Jesus. You will learn what the disciples said. Who do you think Jesus is?**

BIBLICAL LESSON

Prepare the following story, adapted from Matthew 15:21-28; 16:13-28; 17:1-9 before you tell it to the children.

Jesus withdrew to the region of Tyre and Sidon. There, a Canaanite woman cried out, "Lord, Son of David, have mercy on me! My daughter suffers terribly from demon-possession."

Jesus did not answer. So the disciples said, "Send her away."

Jesus replied, "I was sent only to the lost sheep of Israel."

The woman continued to cry out to Jesus. Then Jesus said, "You have great faith! Your request is granted."

When Jesus came to the region of Caesarea Philippi, he asked his disciples, "Who do people say the Son of Man is?"

They replied, "John the Baptist, Elijah, Jeremiah, or another prophet."

Jesus asked the disciples, "Who do you say that I am?"

Simon Peter answered, "You are the Christ, the Son of the living God."

Jesus replied, "Blessed are you. This was not revealed to you by man, but by my Father in heaven. You are Peter, and on this rock I will build my church."

Jesus began to explain to his disciples that he must go to Jerusalem, suffer, be killed, and be raised to life on the third day.

Peter said, "This shall never happen to you!"

Jesus replied, "You do not know the things of God, but the things of men."

Then Jesus said to his disciples, "If anyone would come after me, he must deny himself and take up his cross and follow me. What good will it be for a man if he gains the whole world, yet forfeits his soul?"

Jesus took Peter, James, and John up a mountain by themselves. There he experienced a transfiguration before them. His face shone like the sun, and his clothes became as white as the light. Moses and Elijah appeared before them. They talked with Jesus.

Peter wanted to build three shelters--one for Jesus, one for Moses, and one for Elijah. Then a bright cloud covered them. A voice from the cloud said, "This is my Son, whom I love; with him I am well pleased. Listen to him!"

The disciples fell facedown to the ground, and they were terrified.

Jesus told them not to tell anyone what they saw until the Son of Man experienced resurrection from the dead.

Encourage the children to answer the following questions. There are no right or wrong answers. These questions will help the children to understand the story and to apply it to their lives.

1. The cities of Tyre and Sidon were far from Galilee. How do you think the woman heard about Jesus' power?
2. If you were the woman, how would you respond to the statements of Jesus in 15:24, 26?
3. How do you think Simon Peter felt when Jesus called him Peter and told him why?
4. Why do you think Jesus took only three disciples with him on the mountain?

Say, What would you do if you told someone who your parents are and he or she did not believe you? How would you prove that you really are the child of your parents? Would you point out similarities in the way you look or act? Would you ask your mom or dad to tell this person that you are telling the truth?

Jesus did all of those things too. Jesus healed many people and multiplied a tiny meal to feed thousands of people. Jesus forgave people their sins, and the disciples even heard God the Father claim Jesus as his Son. God told us to listen to Jesus because he is the Son of God.

MEMORY VERSE

Practice the study's memory verse. You will find suggestions for Memory Verse Activities on pages 137-138.

ADDITIONAL ACTIVITIES

Choose from any of these options to enhance the children's Bible study.

1. Do some research about the three disciples that Jesus took on the mountain with him. Search for other stories about Peter, James, and John in the other three Gospels and in the book of Acts. What roles did they play in each story?

2. Have a special speaker prepare a monologue from Peter's perspective about the events in this study's scripture passages. Have this person present the monologue as Peter. Give students the opportunity to ask "Peter" questions.

QUESTIONS FOR BASIC COMPETITION

To prepare the children for competition, read Matthew 15:21-28; 16:13-28; 17:1-9 to them.

1 Why did not Jesus help the Canaanite woman at first? (15:24)
   1. **She was not from Israel.**
   2. To heal her daughter was too difficult for Jesus.
   3. She did not have enough faith.

2 Why did Jesus heal the woman's daughter? (15:28)
   1. She threatened him.
   2. **She had great faith.**
   3. She was a friend of one of the disciples.

3 What was the first question that Jesus asked his disciples in Caesarea Philippi? (16:13)
   1. "What does John the Baptist think about me?"
   2. "Why does Herod not like me?"
   3. **"Who do the people say that the Son of Man is?"**

4 Who did some people think Jesus was? (16:14)
   1. John the Baptist
   2. Elijah or Jeremiah
   3. **Both answers are correct.**

5 How did Peter answer when Jesus asked, "Who do you say I am?" (16:15-16)
   1. **"You are the Christ, the Son of the living God."**
   2. "You are a great teacher and a prophet."
   3. Both answers are correct.

6 From where did Jesus say that Peter got the answer to the question, "Who do you say I am?" (16:15-17)
   1. The other disciples
   2. His mother-in-law
   3. **His Father in heaven**

7 What did Jesus tell the disciples that a person who wants to come after him must do? (16:24)
   1. "He must go to another country.'"
   2. "He must become a teacher."
   3. **"He must deny himself and take up his cross."**

8 What happened on the mountain when Jesus experienced transfiguration? (17:2-3)
   1. The face of Jesus shone like the sun.
   2. Moses and Elijah appeared.
   3. **Both answers are correct.**

9 What did Peter want to do for Jesus, Elijah, and Moses? (17:4)
   1. To build three shelters for James, John, and himself
   2. **To build three shelters, one for each of them**
   3. To build one shelter for everyone

10 What did Jesus say to Peter, James, and John after the voice from the cloud spoke to them? (17:6-7, 9)
   1. "Get up. . . . Don't be afraid."
   2. "Don't tell anyone what you have seen."
   3. **Both answers are correct.**

QUESTIONS FOR ADVANCED COMPETITION

To prepare the children for competition, read Matthew 15:21-28; 16:13-28; 17:1-9 to them.

1 Why did the Canaanite woman cry out to Jesus? (15:22)
   1. She was hungry for something to eat.
   2. **Her daughter suffered from demon-possession.**
   3. She tried to get a special blessing from Jesus.
   4. All of the above

2 What did Jesus ask the disciples when they arrived in the region of Caesarea Philippi? (16:13)
   1. "Will you follow me no matter what happens?"
   2. **"Who do the people say the Son of Man is?"**
   3. "When will the Son of God appear?"
   4. "Who is the Messiah?"

3 What did Peter say when Jesus asked, "Who do you say I am?" (16:15-16)
   1. **"You are the Christ, the Son of the living God."**
   2. "You are a great prophet."
   3. "You are Elijah."
   4. "You are the son of Joseph and Mary."

4 After the disciples acknowledged that Jesus was the Christ, what did Jesus say would happen to him? (16:21)
   1. He would go to Jerusalem and suffer many things.
   2. He must be killed.
   3. After he died, he would be raised to life on the third day.
   4. **All of the above**

5 Why was Peter a stumbling block? (16:23)
   1. Peter was a coward.
   2. **Peter had the things of people in mind, not the things of God.**
   3. Peter always wanted to be first.
   4. Peter never followed the teachings of Jesus.

6 What will happen to the person who loses his or her life for Jesus? (16:25)
   1. He or she will receive power.
   2. He or she will become famous.
   3. He or she will die.
   4. **He or she will find it.**

7 What happened when Jesus took Peter, James, and John up a high mountain by themselves? (17:1-2)
   1. "He experienced the transfiguration before them."
   2. "His face shone like the sun."
   3. "His clothes became as white as the light."
   4. **All of the above**

8 Who appeared with Jesus during his transfiguration? (17:3)
   1. Abraham and Sarah
   2. Gideon and Deborah
   3. **Moses and Elijah**
   4. Joshua and Isaiah

9 What happened while Peter spoke about building three shelters? (17:4-5)
   1. **A voice from a cloud said, "This is my Son, whom I love; with him I am well pleased. Listen to him!"**
   2. James and John started to build the shelters.
   3. Peter met Elijah and Moses.
   4. Moses and Elijah disappeared.

10 Finish this verse: "Simon Peter answered, 'You are the Christ, . . .'" (Matthew 16:16)
   1. "'. . . my Redeemer and friend.'"
   2. **"'. . . the Son of the living God.'"**
   3. "'. . . our teacher and prophet.'"
   4. "'. . . the one who leads us.'"

twelve

Matthew 18:10-14, 21-35; 19:13-30

Memory Verse

"Jesus said, 'Let the little children come to me, and do not hinder them, for the kingdom of heaven belongs to such as these'" (Matthew 19:14).

Biblical Truth

Jesus forgives people and shows concern for them, and we must do the same.

Focus

This lesson will help children learn that we should care for people, because Jesus cares for us.

Teaching Tip

As you lead the Bible study, explain that we need to live our lives in surrender to God. Our treasure is in heaven, not on earth.

BIBLICAL COMMENTARY

In this lesson, we learn about the concern of Jesus for others. In the first passage, Jesus told a parable about a shepherd who left his 99 sheep to find one that was lost. In this story "little ones" refer to believers who have wandered from their faith in God. God makes every effort to save those who become lost. We, as believers, should have this same concern and rejoice over the believers who return to their faith in God.

In the next passage, Jesus and Peter discussed forgiveness. The Jews considered that it was sufficient to forgive someone three times. Peter, a Jew, suggested that it was sufficient to forgive someone seven times. Peter was probably shocked when Jesus said we must forgive someone 77 times. Jesus taught the disciples how important it is to forgive others because Jesus forgives us.

The third and fourth passages deal with people who were at opposite ends of the hierarchy of society. Children were low in the social hierarchy. Jesus wanted his disciples to value children and to have a faith like a child in spiritual matters.

The rich man was high in social standing because of his wealth. However, he did not have the most important blessing--he did not know how to have eternal life.

Our social standing means nothing to Jesus. What is important is to have a heart like Jesus.

CHARACTERISTICS OF GOD

- God seeks the people who do not follow him.
- God forgives us of our sins, and he wants us to do the same thing for other people.

WORDS OF OUR FAITH

Eternal life is the special kind of life God gives to those who trust Jesus as Saviour. Those who trust Jesus will enjoy eternal life forever in heaven.

THINGS

A **talent** was a weight of money, about 34 kg of metal, probably silver.

A **denarius** was a coin that was commonly a day's wages.

To **rebuke** is to tell someone harshly not to do something.

To **hinder** is to block the way.

ACTIVITY

You will need these items for this activity:

- Index cards or pieces of paper
- A toy sheep or a paper sheep

Before class, create some clues to help the children to find a lost sheep. Write one clue that will lead to the next one, until the final clue leads to the lost sheep. Hide the clues in other parts of the facility, if possible. Bring the first clue with you into the class.

Say, **We will read a parable of Jesus about a lost sheep. Today, we will find a lost sheep. Here is a clue that will help us.**

As a class, follow the different clues. Allow the children to solve the clues. Do not tell them the answers. When you find the sheep, return to the classroom.

Say, **Today we found a lost sheep. Now, we will read a parable about a man who found a lost sheep.**

BIBLICAL LESSON

Prepare the following story, adapted from Matthew 18:10-14, 21-35; 19:13-30, before you tell it to the children.

Jesus told many parables to the people around him.

Jesus said, "Do not look down on young children. The angels of these children see the face of God."

Jesus told a parable about a shepherd and his sheep. "A man owned one hundred sheep, and one of the sheep wandered away. He left the other ninety-nine sheep, and he went to find the one lost sheep. When he found the sheep, he was happier that he found that one sheep, than he was about the other ninety-nine sheep that did not wander. In a similar way, God does not want anyone to be lost in sin."

Jesus talked to Peter about forgiveness. Peter said to Jesus, "Lord, how many times must I forgive my brother when he sins against me? Is seven times sufficient?"

Jesus said, "Not seven times, but seventy-seven times."

Then Jesus told a parable about forgiveness. "The kingdom of heaven is like a king. This king wanted to collect the money that people owed to him. He brought to himself a servant who owed him ten thousand talents. The servant was unable to pay his debt. The king ordered that this family should live in the prison until the servant could pay his debt. The servant fell on his knees, and he said 'Be patient with me, and I will pay my debt.' The king felt mercy for the man, so he cancelled the debt and released the servant.

"The servant later met another servant who owed him a hundred denarii. The first servant grabbed the second servant and began to choke him. He said, 'Pay back what you owe me!'

The second servant said, 'Be patient, and I will pay you back.' However, the first servant refused. He sent the second servant to the prison. The other servants saw what happened, and they told their master about it.

The master called the servant to come to him. The master said, 'You wicked servant! I cancelled your debt. You should have mercy on your fellow servant.' The master was angry, and he sent the wicked servant to the prison. The servant received torture until he could pay his debt. This is how God will treat you unless you forgive people who do wrong actions against you."

Some people brought children to Jesus, so that Jesus could pray for them. The disciples rebuked those who brought the children. However, Jesus said, "Let the children come to me. The kingdom of heaven belongs to people like them."

A man came to Jesus and asked, "What should I do to earn eternal life?"

Jesus said, "If you want eternal life, you must obey the commandments."

The man said, "I already keep all of the commandments. What must I do beyond this?"

Jesus said, "Sell all of your possessions and give the money to the poor people. Then you will have treasure in heaven." The young man went away. He was sad, because he was extremely wealthy.

Jesus said, "It is difficult for a wealthy man to enter the kingdom of heaven."

The disciples said, "If that is true, who can be saved?"

Jesus said, "With man this is impossible, but with God all things are possible."

Peter asked, "We left everything we have to follow you. What will we receive?"

Jesus said, "Everyone who left their families and their homes will receive a reward that has one hundred times more worth. He will inherit eternal life. Many who are first will be last, and many who are last will be first."

Encourage the children to answer the following questions. There may not be a right or wrong answer. These questions help the children to understand the story and to apply it to their lives.

1. Have you ever lost something that was valuable? What did you do to find what you lost? How did you feel when you found it? Why did the shepherd value the lost sheep so much?

2. How did the wicked servant feel when the king forgave his debt? How did the king feel when he saw what the wicked servant did? Has someone forgiven you for something wrong that you did?

3. The rich young man was sad because he did not want to give up his wealth. What are some things that people think are difficult to give up to God?

Say, **Have you ever fought about who gets to be first or whose turn is next? Too often we focus only on our needs. Jesus showed concern about the needs of others. Jesus invited the children to gather around him even when the disciples protested. Jesus has a heart of love for everyone, and he offers forgiveness to everyone. Do you love others and offer forgiveness to others?**

MEMORY VERSE

Practice the study's memory verse. You will find suggestions for Memory Verse Activities on pages 137-138.

ADDITIONAL ACTIVITIES

Choose from these options to enhance the children's Bible study.

1. As a class, act out the parable of the lost sheep. Choose students to be the herd of sheep, one student to be the lost sheep, and one student to be the shepherd. The lost sheep will hide, and the shepherd can find that sheep.

2. Jesus told the rich young man to sell his possessions, give to the poor, and follow him. As a class, make a list of possessions that people may have that might hinder their relationship with God. What are some ways to overcome these hindrances?

QUESTIONS FOR BASIC COMPETITION

To prepare the children for competition, read Matthew 18:10-14, 21-35; 19:13-30 to them.

1 According to the parable of Jesus, how many sheep did the man own? (18:12)
   1. **100**
   2. 500
   3. 1000

2 What did the man do when he realized that one sheep was gone? (18:12)
   1. He forgot about the lost sheep.
   2. **He went to look for the sheep.**
   3. He sent someone else to look for the sheep.

3 What question did Peter ask Jesus about forgiveness? (18:21)
   1. "Do I need forgiveness?"
   2. "Who needs forgiveness?"
   3. **"How many times shall I forgive?"**

4 How much did the first servant owe the king? (18:23-24)
   1. **10,000 talents**
   2. 1,000 talents
   3. 10 talents

5 What did the king do when the servant asked the king to show patience? (18:26-27)
   1. The king took pity on the servant.
   2. The king cancelled the debt, and he let the servant go.
   3. **Both answers are correct.**

6 What did the first servant do to the servant who owed him money? (18:30)
   1. **He demanded that he repay him.**
   2. He forgave the servant.
   3. Both answers are correct.

7 What did the king do when he learned what the first servant did? (18:32-34)
   1. He let him go.
   2. **He called him a wicked servant, and he turned him over to the jailers.**
   3. He told him that he did the right thing.

8 What did Jesus tell the disciples about the children? (19:14)
   1. "Let the little children come to me."
   2. "The kingdom of heaven belongs to such as these."
   3. **Both answers are correct.**

9 What did Jesus say to the man who asked, "What good thing must I do to receive eternal life?" (19:17)
   1. **"Obey the commandments."**
   2. "Study the scriptures."
   3. "Go to the synagogue every week."

10 Who said, "With man this is impossible, but with God all things are possible"? (19:26)
   1. Peter
   2. **Jesus**
   3. The rich young man

QUESTIONS FOR ADVANCED COMPETITION

To prepare the children for competition, read Matthew 18:10-14, 21-35; 19:13-30 to them.

1 Who always sees the face of the Father in heaven? (18:10)
   1. **The angels of the little ones**
   2. No one
   3. Those who forgive others
   4. Everyone

2 What did Jesus say was the meaning of the parable of the lost sheep? (18:14)
   1. "It is your fault if you get lost."
   2. "It is easy to get lost in the forest."
   3. **"Your Father in heaven is not willing that any of these little ones should be lost."**
   4. "Stay with the flock. Do not get lost."

3 How many times did Jesus say to forgive? (18:22)
   1. 3 times
   2. 7 times
   3. **77 times**
   4. 700 times

4 What did the first servant do when the king told him to repay his debt? (18:25-26)
   1. He repaid the debt of a fellow servant.
   2. He ran away.
   3. He repaid his debt.
   4. **He begged the king for patience.**

5 How much did the second servant owe to the first servant? (18:28)
   1. **100 denarii**
   2. 1,000 denarii
   3. 1,000 talents
   4. 10,000 talents

6 What did the servants do when they saw what the first servant did to the second servant? (18:31)
   1. They told the first servant that he did the right thing.
   2. **They told the king what happened.**
   3. They did nothing.
   4. They raised money for the servant.

7 What did Jesus tell the disciples when they rebuked the people who brought little children to him? (19:13-14)
   1. "Let the little children come to me."
   2. "Do not hinder them."
   3. "The kingdom of heaven belongs to such as these."
   4. **All of the above**

8 What did Jesus do when the little children came to him? (19:13-15)
   1. He blessed each family.
   2. **He placed his hands on them and prayed for them.**
   3. He baptized them.
   4. He turned them away.

9 What did the young man do when Jesus told him what he should do to receive eternal life? (19:22)
   1. He became a disciple of Jesus.
   2. **He went away sad, because he had great wealth.**
   3. He sold all that he possessed, and he gave the money to the poor.
   4. He asked why God had so many rules.

10 Finish this verse: "Jesus said, 'Let the little children come to me, and do not...'" (Matthew 19:14)
   1. **"'...hinder them, for the kingdom of heaven belongs to such as these.'"**
   2. "'...punish them harshly.'"
   3. "'...let them run away from me.'"
   4. "'...allow them to stray.'"

thirteen

Matthew 21:1-17; 22:34-40

Memory Verse

"Jesus replied: 'Love the Lord your God with all your heart and with all your soul and with all your mind. This is the first and greatest commandment. And the second is like it: Love your neighbour as yourself'" (Matthew 22:37-39).

Biblical Truth

Jesus, our Saviour and King, is worthy of our praise, our obedience, and our love.

Focus

In this lesson, children will learn that Jesus said that the greatest commandment is to love the Lord our God completely. The second greatest commandment is to love our neighbours as ourselves.

Teaching Tip

See Lesson 2 for a definition of a Pharisee and a Sadducee.

BIBLICAL COMMENTARY

When Jesus entered Jerusalem on a donkey, the crowd recognized this action as a sign that Jesus was the king for whom they waited. To ride into a city in this way was a common practice for the kings during Old Testament times. In recognition of this, the people called Jesus the "Son of David." This was another name for the Messiah. The people were correct to call Jesus a king. However, they expected him to be an earthly king. They thought he would defeat their political enemies. They did not know that he would suffer a crucifixion for their sins.

When Jesus entered the Temple, he was angry because people turned a place of worship into a marketplace. They sold animals for the sacrifices, and they exchanged money for Temple offerings. These booths and these services were necessary. However, their placement and the dishonest business practices of some of the people showed disrespect to the Temple and to the people who were there to worship. When Jesus took charge, the people saw his authority. The chief priests saw this as a challenge to their authority.

In Bible times, it was not unusual for religious people to argue about which commandments were more important. Jesus said the most important commandment is to love God with all that you are. The second is to love your neighbour; this love flows out of a love for God.

CHARACTERISTICS OF GOD

- Jesus is worthy of our praise.
- God wants us to love him and to love others.

PLACES

The **Mount of Olives** is a mountain east of Jerusalem that is 823 meters tall. From the peak, there is a great view of Jerusalem and the Temple.

A **temple** is a building for the worship of a god or gods. The Jerusalem Temple was a place where the Jews worshiped God.

Bethany was a village about 3.3 kilometres east of Jerusalem, near the Mount of Olives

THINGS

A **cloak** is a loose outer garment.

ACTIVITY

You will need these items for this activity:

- A large sheet of paper
- Some markers

Before class, print the word, "Hosanna," in large letters on a large sheet of paper.

During class, point to the word "Hosanna" and say, **Today we will learn about a time when people shouted "Hosanna!" to Jesus. What do you think "Hosanna" means?** (It means "Save!" It is also an exclamation of praise.) **What are some ways we can show praise for Jesus?**

Encourage the children to draw some pictures or to write some words around the large letters. The pictures or the words should express some ways that the children will praise Jesus. Display the poster in the classroom.

BIBLICAL LESSON

Prepare the following story, adapted from Matthew 21:1-17; 22:34-40 before you tell it to the children.

As Jesus and his disciples approached Jerusalem, they came to Bethpage on the Mount of Olives. Jesus sent ahead two disciples.

Jesus said to the two disciples, "Go to the village ahead of you, and at once you will find a donkey tied there, with her colt by her. Untie them and bring them to me. If anyone says anything to you, tell him that the Lord needs them." All of this fulfilled the words of the prophet that said, "See, your king comes to you, gentle and riding on a donkey."

The disciples brought the donkey and the colt. The disciples placed their cloaks on them, and Jesus sat on the cloaks. A very large crowd spread their cloaks on the road, while other people cut tree branches and spread them on the road.

The crowds shouted, "Hosanna to the Son of David!" "Blessed is he who comes in the name of the Lord!" "Hosanna in the highest!"

When Jesus entered Jerusalem, the whole city asked, "Who is this?"

The crowds answered, "This is Jesus, the prophet from Nazareth in Galilee."

Then Jesus entered the Temple area. He drove out the people who bought and sold there. He overturned the tables of the money changers and the benches of the people who sold doves. Jesus said, "My house will be called a house of prayer, but you are making it a den of robbers."

Jesus healed the blind people and the lame people who came to him at the Temple. The chief priests and the teachers of the Law saw the wonderful things that Jesus did. They heard the children who shouted "Hosanna to the Son of David," and they became angry.

"Do you hear what these children said?" they asked Jesus.

"Yes," replied Jesus, "have you never read, 'From the lips of children and infants you have ordained praise'?"

Then Jesus left, and he went to Bethany.

The Pharisees tried to test Jesus. An expert in the law asked, "Teacher, which is the greatest commandment in the Law?"

Jesus replied, "Love the Lord your God with all your heart and with all your soul and with all your mind. This is the first and greatest commandment. And the second is like it: Love your neighbour as yourself. All the Law and the Prophets hang on these two commandments."

Encourage the children to answer the following questions. There are no right or wrong answers. These questions will help the children to understand the story and to apply it to their lives.

1. Why did Jesus tell his disciples to go to another town to find a donkey and a colt for him to ride?
2. What praises did the people give to Jesus? What kind of praises would you give to Jesus?
3. What did the money changers do that Jesus did not like?
4. Do you think that the Pharisees knew what the greatest commandment was? If they did, why did they ask Jesus what it was?
5. What two commandments did Jesus give in Matthew 22:37-39? Why is it important for you to obey these commandments?

Say, Jesus did not do anything in the way that the Jews expected of the King of Kings. He rode into the town on a donkey. The men, the women, and the children praised him. Jesus did not act grandly or gloriously, yet Jesus possessed the authority of God. Jesus was worthy of their praise. Jesus modelled how to love God with the whole self. He also modelled how to love others as we love our own self. We should follow his example. We should love, obey, and worship God.

MEMORY VERSE

Practice the study's memory verse. You will find suggestions for Memory Verse

Activities on pages 137-138.

ADDITIONAL ACTIVITIES

Choose from any of these options to enhance the children's Bible study.

1. In Bible times, kings would enter their cities triumphantly after they won a battle. Research what would take place during these "Triumphal Entries." Compare and contrast what you find with the Triumphal Entry of Jesus. What is the symbolism behind the action of the people to put their cloaks and tree branches in the road?

2. Imagine that Jesus rode into your town. What kinds of things would people say about him? How would your town welcome him? What kinds of praises would you give him? Draw a map of the route Jesus would take if he came to your town. Create a banner to announce his arrival. Then thank God that he sent Jesus to save us.

QUESTIONS FOR BASIC COMPETITION

To prepare the children for competition, read Matthew 21:1-17; 22:34-40 to them.

1 What did Jesus ask two disciples to do when they came to Bethphage? (21:1-2)
  1. **"Go to the village, find a donkey and colt, and bring them to me."**
  2. "Find a place for us to spend the night."
  3. "Go ahead of me to see if Herod will arrest us."

2 What were the disciples to say if anyone said anything to them about the donkey and the colt? (21:3)
  1. "These are our animals."
  2. **"The Lord needs them."**
  3. "May we take your donkeys?"

3 What did the Old Testament prophecy say about the disciples and the colt and the donkey? (21:2-5)
  1. "See, your king comes to you."
  2. He is "gentle and riding on a donkey."
  3. **Both answers are correct.**

4 What did the crowd do when Jesus rode into Jerusalem? (21:8-9)
  1. They spread their cloaks and tree branches on the road.
  2. They shouted, "Hosanna to the Son of David!"
  3. **Both answers are correct.**

5 What did the people sell in the Temple area? (21:12)
  1. **Doves**
  2. Incense
  3. Scrolls

6 What did Jesus do in the Temple area after he entered Jerusalem? (21:12)
  1. He drove out those who bought and those who sold.
  2. He turned over the tables of the money changers.
  3. **Both answers are correct.**

7 What did Jesus say that the people did to the house of prayer? (21:13)
  1. **Made it a den of robbers**
  2. Made it a place of worship
  3. Made it a market

8 What did Jesus do after he drove out the people who bought and sold in the Temple? (21:12, 14)
  1. He took an offering for the altar.
  2. **He healed those who came to him.**
  3. He went to Nazareth.

9 Who tested Jesus with a question about the greatest commandment? (22:35-36)
  1. One of the disciples
  2. **An expert in the Law**
  3. King Herod

10 What did Jesus say is the second greatest commandment? (22:39)
  1. "Do not take the name of God in vain."
  2. **"Love your neighbour as yourself."**
  3. "Honour your father and your mother."

QUESTIONS FOR ADVANCED COMPETITION

To prepare the children for competition, read Matthew 21:1-17; 22:34-40 to them.

1 What did Jesus do at Bethphage? (21:1-2)
1. He prayed and fasted.
2. **He sent two of his disciples to find a donkey and a colt.**
3. He healed the sick.
4. He told the parable of the unmerciful servant.

2 What did the disciples do with the donkeys? (21:7)
1. They took them back to Nazareth.
2. They rode them into Jerusalem.
3. **They placed their cloaks on the donkeys for Jesus to ride on them.**
4. They sold them to pay the tax for the Temple.

3 What did the large crowd do when Jesus rode into Jerusalem? (21:8-9)
1. **They spread their cloaks and tree branches on the road.**
2. They threw rocks at him.
3. They walked away from the city.
4. All of the above

4 When Jesus entered Jerusalem, how did the crowd answer the question: "Who is this?"? (21:11)
1. "Jesus, the Son of Mary and Joseph."
2. "The Messiah"
3. **"Jesus, the prophet from Nazareth in Galilee"**
4. "The new king of Jerusalem"

5 What did Jesus say when he overturned the tables of the money changers and the people who sold doves? (21:13)
1. **"My house will be called a house of prayer, but you are making it a 'den of robbers.'"**
2. "All who cheat the innocent will die!"
3. "The day of judgment has come."
4. All of the above

6 What did Jesus do when the lame people and the blind people came to him in the Temple? (21:14)
1. He took them to the high priest.
2. He asked them to bring a sacrifice.
3. **He healed them.**
4. He told them to wash in the Jordan River.

7 What did the children shout in the Temple area? (21:15)
1. **"Hosanna to the Son of David."**
2. "Glory to God in the highest."
3. "The Prince of Peace has come."
4. "The Holy One is come."

8 What did Jesus say when the chief priests and the teachers of the Law asked Jesus about the shouts of the children? (21:16)
1. "Leave the children alone."
2. **"Have you never read: 'From the lips of children and infants you have ordained praise'?"**
3. "The children are the prophets of the one who has come."
4. "Children are the voice of God."

9 What did Jesus say is the greatest commandment in the Law? (22:37-38)
1. **"Love the Lord your God with all your heart and with all your soul and with all your mind."**
2. "Remember the Sabbath day to keep it holy."
3. "You shall have no other gods before the Lord your God."
4. "Do not misuse the name of the Lord your God."

10 According to Jesus, what hangs on the two great commandments? (22:40)
1. The Sermon on the Mount
2. The Golden Rule
3. **The Law and the Prophets**
4. The Beatitudes

fourteen

Matthew 24:36-42; 25:1-30

Memory Verse

"'Because of the increase of wickedness, the love of most will grow cold, but he who stands firm to the end will be saved'" (Matthew 24:12-13).

Biblical Truth

Jesus will come again. His followers prepare for this event.

Focus

This lesson will help the children learn that we need to prepare for the return of Jesus.

Teaching Tip

As you lead the Bible study, remind the children that if they follow God, they do not need to fear the future. God wants his followers to have joy and to have faith in him.

BIBLICAL COMMENTARY

Only God the Father knows when Jesus will return. Although that may upset some people, it is a reminder to us to follow the commands of God. We are to forgive others and to prepare for his return. These two parables give us a picture of our lives when Jesus returns.

Weddings were important in Jewish society. A wedding required the groom to meet first with the father of the bride. Then, unmarried women would lead the groom by torch light to his house for a wedding feast. In the parable, all ten virgins fell asleep while they waited for the groom. When the groom arrived, only five of the virgins were prepared. Because of this, only those five virgins led the groom to the feast. The groom locked the door, and the other virgins could not come inside.

The second parable is an illustration of God and his relationship with each of us. One talent was a small fortune. The master gave different amounts of money to different servants. To each servant he gave an amount that was equivalent to the ability of the servant. The servant who did not want to risk the loss of his talent did nothing with the one talent. In the end, that servant lost everything.

From these parables, we realize that it is important to prepare ourselves for the return of Christ. We also understand that God wants us to use our talents to serve him and to build his kingdom.

CHARACTERISTICS OF GOD

- God knows when Jesus will return, and he wants us to prepare for his return.
- God prepares us to do his work.

WORDS OF OUR FAITH

The **Second Coming** is the time when Jesus will return to earth. Jesus will reign, and there will be no evil.

PEOPLE

The **ten virgins** were young women who were friends or family members of the bride or groom.

The **bridegroom** was the man who would marry the bride at the wedding.

Other New Testament Terms

Lamps were clay pots with spouts. People poured the oil into the pot, and they placed a wick in the spout.

To **trim** a lamp meant to cut off the burnt end of the wick.

Interest is the extra money that you earn on the money that you deposited into a bank.

ACTIVITY

You will need these items for this activity:

- Some paper plates, one for each child who plays the game. If you do not have any paper plates, use any set of identical objects.
- A sticker or marker

Before the class begins, mark the bottom of one of the plates with the sticker or marker. Display the plates where the children can see them. Give each child a number. Start at one, and continue to count in sequence until each child has a number.

Say, **Today, we will read a parable about a wedding. Some of the people at the wedding brought some lamps that did not have sufficient oil. In this activity, these plates represent different lamps that you can bring to the wedding. One of these lamps does not have sufficient oil. That lamp has a mark on the bottom.**

You received a number. In numerical order, select one of the lamps. When everyone selects a lamp, we will check to see who has the lamp without any oil. That person is out of the game.

After you identify the lamp without oil, remove one of the plates without a mark. Randomize the plates that remain. The children who remain will select another plate. However, this time, go in reverse numerical order. The child with the highest number selects the first plate. Continue in descending numerical order until all of the children select a plate. Alternate the numerical order for each round, until only one child remains. That child wins the game.

Say, **When you selected a lamp that had no oil, you could not continue in the game. Today, we will hear a parable that**

Jesus told about some people who did not bring enough oil for their lamps. We will learn what happened to them.

BIBLICAL LESSON

Prepare the following story, adapted from Matthew 24:36-42; 25:1-30, before you tell it to the children.

Jesus preached to his followers. He said, "No one knows when the end times will come. Only the Father knows this information. When the Son of Man comes, it will be like it was in the time of Noah. Before the flood came, people ate, drank, and continued their lives. They knew nothing of the flood until it came and took them away. This is how it will be when the Son of Man comes. Be vigilant, because no one knows when the end times will come.

"The end times will be like ten virgins who took their lamps to a wedding. Five of the virgins were wise, and they brought extra oil for their lamps. Five of the virgins were foolish, and they brought no extra oil. The bridegroom did not come for a long time, and the virgins fell asleep.

"At midnight, the virgins went to meet the bridegroom. They woke up, and they trimmed their lamps. The foolish virgins had no more oil, so they asked for some oil from the wise virgins. The wise virgins said, 'If we give you some oil, we will not have enough for ourselves. Go and buy some oil for yourselves.'

"While they bought the oil, the bridegroom arrived. The virgins who were ready for him went to the wedding banquet, and they shut the door. The other virgins returned with their oil. They said, 'Let us in! Open the door for us!'

"The host said, 'I do not know you.'"

Jesus said, "Therefore, be vigilant. No one knows when the end times will come."

Jesus told another parable. "A man went on a journey. He entrusted some property to his servants. The first servant received five talents. The second servant received two talents. The final servant received only one talent. The first servant invested his money, and he gained five more talents. The second servant also invested his money, and he gained two more talents. The man who received one talent buried his talent in the ground.

"The master returned, and he asked about the money that he gave to the servants. The servant who received the five talents brought five additional talents. The master said, 'Well done! You have been faithful with the things that I gave you. I will place you in the command of many things.'

"The second servant brought the two talents and two additional talents. The master said, 'Well done! You have done well with a few things. Come and share in the happiness of your master.'

The third servant said, 'Master, I was afraid of you. Because of this, I hid your talent in the ground. Here is your money.'

The master replied, 'You wicked servant! You should have put my money in the bank. I could collect interest on my money. I will take your talent, and I will give it to the servant with ten talents. Everyone who has will receive more, and he will have an abundance. Throw this servant outside, where there is darkness.'"

Encourage the children to answer the following questions. There are no right or wrong answers. These questions help the children to understand the story and to apply it to their lives.

1. **The five foolish virgins could not go into the wedding. How do you think they felt about their exclusion?**
2. **Many people tried to predict when Jesus will return. Why do people feel the need to predict this event?**
3. **Why was the servant with one talent afraid of the master? Did you ever do something because you were afraid of a person?**

Say, **Did you ever help your parents to prepare for a visitor? What kinds of jobs did you do? Was everything ready by the** time that your visitor arrived? When Jesus left this earth to go back to heaven, he promised that he would return. He went to prepare a place for us. We do not know when he will return. However, Jesus will come again to take to heaven those who asked for forgiveness of their sin and who follow him. Jesus challenges us to obey and to prepare for his return. How can you prepare for the second coming of Jesus?

MEMORY VERSE

Practice the study's memory verse. You will find suggestions for Memory Verse Activities on pages 137-138.

ADDITIONAL ACTIVITIES

1. As a class, discuss the Parable of the Talents. Even though the talents in the story refer to money, discuss how we use our gifts and talents. How can we use our talents to glorify God?

2. As a class, research how people used lamps in the time of Jesus. Let each child draw a lamp.

QUESTIONS FOR BASIC COMPETITION

To prepare the children for competition, read Matthew 24:36-42; 25:1-30 to them.

1 Jesus said that the Lord will come when we do not expect Him. What should we do? (24:42)
1. **Keep watch.**
2. Do nothing but wait.
3. Both answers are correct.

2 Why did the ten virgins take their lamps and go out? (25:1)
1. To see what happened
2. **To meet the bridegroom**
3. To meet the family of the bridegroom

3 Why were five of the virgins wise? (25:4)
1. **They took lamps and oil with them.**
2. They knew exactly when the bridegroom would come.
3. Both answers are correct.

4 How did the wise virgins answer the foolish virgins when they asked for oil? (25:9)
1. "There may not be enough for both us and you."
2. "Go to those who sell oil, and buy some for yourselves."
3. **Both answers are correct.**

5 What happened while the foolish virgins went to buy the oil? (25:10)
1. The wise virgins ran out of oil.
2. **The bridegroom came.**
3. The wise virgins fell asleep.

6 What did the man with one talent do with his money? (25:18)
1. He gained one more talent.
2. He put his money in the bank.
3. **He dug a hole and buried his talent.**

7 When the master returned, what did the man who received five talents say? (25:20)
1. "I am sorry. I wasted your money."
2. **"See, I have gained five more."**
3. "I put your money in the bank."

8 What did the master say to the servant who earned five more talents? (25:21)
1. "Well done, good and faithful servant!"
2. "You have been faithful with a few things; I will put you in charge of many things."
3. **Both answers are correct.**

9 What did the master say to the man who had gained two more talents? (25:23)
1. **"Come and share your master's happiness!"**
2. "You should give your talents away."
3. "Come and enjoy a banquet in your honour!"

10 What did the master say to the man who hid his one talent in the ground? (25:26-27)
1. "You wicked, lazy servant!"
2. "You should have put my money on deposit with the bankers."
3. **Both answers are correct.**

QUESTIONS FOR ADVANCED COMPETITION

To prepare the children for competition, read Matthew 24:36-42; 25:1-30 to them.

1 Who knows the day and the hour of the second coming of Christ? (24:36)
1. The angels
2. **The Father**
3. Pastors
4. Jesus

2 Why are you to keep watch and prepare? (24:42)
1. **No one knows when the Lord will come.**
2. People will try to rob your home.
3. You might be in an accident.
4. There are many tasks that we must do.

3 What did the virgins do when the bridegroom took a long time to come? (25:5)
1. They looked for the bridegroom.
2. They kept each other awake.
3. They looked for some things to do.
4. **They fell asleep.**

4 What cry rang out at midnight? (25:6)
1. "Wake up! The bridegroom is almost here."
2. **"Here's the bridegroom! Come out to meet him!"**
3. "Light your lamps!"
4. "Go buy your oil quickly! The bridegroom is coming."

5 What did the virgins do when they heard the cry at midnight? (25:6-7)
1. All of them continued to sleep.
2. The wise virgins woke up the foolish virgins.
3. **They woke up, and they trimmed their lamps.**
4. The wise virgins woke up, and the foolish virgins slept.

6 What happened while the foolish virgins went to buy oil? (25:10)
1. The bridegroom arrived.
2. The virgins who were ready went in with him to the wedding banquet.
3. The door was shut.
4. **All of the above**

7 How many talents of money did the master give to his servants? (25:15)
1. **To one servant, he gave five talents of the money. To another, he gave two talents, and the last servant received one talent.**
2. He gave 10 talents to one servant and five talents to each of the other two servants.
3. He gave each servant 10 talents.
4. He gave each servant 5 talents.

8 What did the man with five talents and the man with two talents do with their money? (25:16-17)
1. They gave their talents to people who had no money.
2. **The man with five talents gained five more talents, and the man with two talents gained two more talents.**
3. They gave their talents to the man with one talent.
4. They did not do anything with their talents.

9 What did the master do with the one talent his servant hid in the ground? (25:25, 28)
1. He gave it to the man with two talents.
2. He put it in the bank.
3. **He gave it to the man with 10 talents.**
4. He gave it to his son.

10 Finish this verse: "Because of the increase of wickedness, the love of most will grow cold, but..." (Matthew 24:12-13)
1. **"...he who stands firm to the end will be saved."**
2. "...God will punish those who do evil."
3. "...they will not know what they do."
4. "...God will remain faithful."

fifteen

Matthew 26:1-30

Memory Verse

"In him we have redemption through his blood, the forgiveness of sins, in accordance with the riches of God's grace" (Ephesians 1:7).

Biblical Truth

Jesus knowingly prepared to give his life for all people.

Focus

In this lesson, the children will learn that Jesus gave new meaning to the bread and the cup.

Teaching Tip

Help the children to understand the significance of each event that happened. Read the Biblical Commentary and do additional research for extra information.

BIBLICAL COMMENTARY

As the time for the death of Jesus approached, he tried to prepare the disciples. Jesus specifically said that he would experience a crucifixion during the time of the Passover celebration. We do not know what the disciples thought about this. Instead, we learn of the actions of the chief priests that verified the words of Jesus. Jesus declared what was about to happen before the chief priests finished their plans.

We also learn of a woman who anointed Jesus with perfume. It was a common burial practice to pour some oil on a body. The disciples viewed the actions of the woman as wasteful actions. Jesus, however, in another attempt to reveal to the disciples that he would experience a crucifixion, praised the woman for her actions. Jesus said that her actions prepared him for the Cross.

In short, the Crucifixion was part of the plan for Jesus. It was not a mistake that caught him by surprise. It was not a death from which he could not escape, although the Jewish and Roman leaders forced it upon him.

Jesus had a clear understanding of the significance of his death and how it fit into the plan of salvation. The sacrificial death of Jesus brought the Passover sacrifice—the blood of the lamb—to its fullness. The Passover meal also symbolized the salvation from God. Jesus used the meal to show that he was the fulfilment of the will of God.

CHARACTERISTICS OF GOD

- Jesus prepared to give his life for all people.
- Jesus taught us to remember him when we take Communion.

WORDS OF OUR FAITH

A **covenant** is an agreement between God and his people. Both God and the people make promises to each other. The **covenants** of God offer us a relationship of love with him.

PEOPLE

The **high priest** was the spiritual leader of the Jewish people.

Caiaphas was the high priest who plotted the arrest of Jesus and who asked for the death of Jesus.

Rabbi is a Jewish word used for a teacher.

PLACES

The **Mount of Olives** was a wooded area similar to a park where people went to escape from the city, the heat, and the crowds in Jerusalem.

OTHER TERMS

Passover is the annual Jewish feast that celebrates the deliverance by God of the Israelites from their slavery in Egypt.

Alabaster is a soft white or light-coloured stone. People carve it to make beautiful vases and small boxes.

BIBLICAL LESSON

Prepare the following story, adapted from Matthew 26:1-30 before you tell it to the children.

Jesus said to his disciples, "The Passover is in two days, and the Son of Man will be handed over for crucifixion."

The chief priests and elders gathered in the palace of Caiaphas, the high priest. They plotted to arrest Jesus and to kill him. "But not during the Feast," they said, "or there may be a riot among the people."

Jesus was in Bethany in the home of Simon the Leper. A woman came to him with an alabaster jar of extremely expensive perfume. She poured it on his head. The disciples said, "We could sell this perfume at a high price, and we could give the money to the poor."

Jesus said, "This woman has done a beautiful thing. When she poured this perfume on my body, she did it to prepare me for burial. Wherever this gospel is preached throughout the world, what she has done will also be told."

Judas Iscariot, one of the twelve disciples, met with the chief priests. He asked, "What will you give me if I hand over Jesus to you?"

The chief priests gave Judas thirty silver coins. Judas watched for an opportunity to hand over Jesus to the chief priests.

On the first day of the Feast of Unleavened Bread, the disciples asked Jesus where he wanted to eat the Passover feast.

Jesus replied, "Go into the city to a certain man and tell him, the Teacher says, I am going to celebrate the Passover with my disciples at your house." The disciples did this, and they prepared the Passover meal.

That evening, Jesus was at the table with the twelve disciples. He said, "One of you will betray me."

They were very sad, and they began to say to him one after the other, "Surely not I, Lord?"

Judas asked, "Surely not I, Rabbi?"

Jesus answered, "Yes, it is you."

Then Jesus took the bread, he gave thanks, he broke the bread, and he gave the bread to his disciples. He said, "Take and eat; this is my body."

Then he took the cup, he gave thanks, and he offered the cup to his disciples. He said, "Drink from it, all of you. This is my blood of the covenant, which is poured out for many for the forgiveness of sins."

They sang a hymn. Then they went to the Mount of Olives.

Encourage the children to answer the following questions. There are no right or wrong answers. These questions will help the children to understand the story and to apply it to their lives.

1. How do you think the disciples felt when Jesus told to them that he would experience a crucifixion, and that the woman prepared him for his burial? Explain your answer.

2. Do you think the disciples were wrong when they became angry at the woman who poured perfume on the head of Jesus? Why or why not?

3. What are some reasons for Judas to betray Jesus? Has a friend ever betrayed you?

4. Imagine you were a disciple at the Passover meal. How would you feel when Jesus told you that a disciple would betray him? How do you think Judas felt when he realized that Jesus knew that the betrayer was Judas?

Say, As the time for Jesus to die became closer, he celebrated the Passover with his disciples. While they ate, Jesus took the bread, and he broke it. Jesus gave the bread to the disciples with instructions that the bread represented his body. Jesus took the cup, and he gave it to them. Jesus said that the wine represented his blood that he gave for the forgiveness of the sins of all people.

Today we speak of the meal as the Lord's Supper or Communion. Christians today participate in the Communion to remember the suffering and the death of Jesus on the Cross. When you take Communion, think about what Jesus did for you. We can receive forgiveness of our sins because Jesus gave his life.

ACTIVITY

Say, **Today we learned about the Passover Feast that Jesus and his disciples shared. During the feast, the Jews ate unleavened bread (bread without yeast) and drank the wine. This symbolized the time when God helped his people escape quickly from Pharaoh** (Exodus 12). **During the Last Supper, Jesus gave new meaning to the bread and the wine. He told his disciples that these elements represented his body and his blood. Today, we take Communion with the bread and the juice to remind us of the sacrifice of Jesus.**

Have your pastor come to speak about Communion and answer any questions that the children have.

MEMORY VERSE

Practice the study's memory verse. You will find suggestions for Memory Verse Activities on pages 137-138.

ADDITIONAL ACTIVITIES

Choose from any of these options to enhance the children's Bible study.

1. Research the New Testament practice of pouring perfume on the head of a person. What was the significance of this? Why was this a part of a burial ritual? Imagine that you are the woman who poured the perfume on the head of Jesus. How do you think she felt before, during, and after she did this? How do you think she responded when Jesus said that people throughout the world would know what she did for him?

2. Make a timeline to outline the events that happened to Jesus in this study. Write or illustrate the following things for each situation: What happened? How did Jesus respond? How do you think he felt about what occurred?

QUESTIONS FOR BASIC COMPETITION

To prepare the children for competition, read Matthew 26:1-30 to them.

1 According to Jesus, who would experience a crucifixion? (26:2)
   1. **The Son of Man**
   2. Peter
   3. The Son of John

2 What was the name of the high priest? (26:3)
   1. Joseph
   2. **Caiaphas**
   3. Pilate

3 In what town did Simon the Leper live? (26:6)
   1. Bethlehem
   2. **Bethany**
   3. Jerusalem

4 What did the woman at the home of Simon the Leper do to Jesus? (26:6-7)
   1. **She poured perfume on his head.**
   2. She bowed as a sign of respect.
   3. She gave him food to eat.

5 How did Jesus describe the action of the woman who poured perfume on him? (26:10)
   1. Mean
   2. **Beautiful**
   3. A waste

6 Whom did Jesus tell the disciples that they would always have with them? (26:11)
   1. **The poor**
   2. The rich
   3. The Son of God

7 How much money did the chief priests give to Judas to hand over Jesus to them? (26:14-15)
   1. 10 gold coins
   2. **30 silver coins**
   3. 40 copper coins

8 What did Jesus say when he broke the bread at the Passover meal? (26:26)
   1. "Eat this bread. We have a long night ahead of us."
   2. "This bread reminds me of our ancestors who fled from the Egyptians."
   3. **"Take and eat; this is my body."**

9 For what reason did Jesus say that he poured out his blood of the covenant? (26:28)
   1. To save his disciples only
   2. **For the forgiveness of sins**
   3. For the sins of his family

10 After Jesus and the disciples sang a hymn at the Passover feast, where did they go? (26:30)
   1. **The Mount of Olives**
   2. The Sea of Galilee
   3. The city of Nazareth

QUESTIONS FOR ADVANCED COMPETITION

To prepare the children for competition, read Matthew 26:1-30 to them.

1 Two days before the Passover, what did Jesus tell his disciples would happen to the Son of Man? (26:2)
1. **Someone would hand over Jesus for his crucifixion.**
2. He would experience a baptism in the Jordan River.
3. He would become the King of Jerusalem.
4. All of the above

2 Why did the chief priests and the elders not want to arrest Jesus during the Feast? (26:4-5)
1. There might be trouble with the Roman guards.
2. There might be children in the town.
3. Innocent people might get hurt.
4. **It might cause a riot among the people.**

3 What did the woman do to Jesus to prepare him for burial? (26:7, 12)
1. She wrapped him in expensive clothing.
2. She washed his feet with some water.
3. **She poured some perfume on his head.**
4. She cut his hair.

4 How did Jesus describe the action of the woman who poured the perfume on him? (26:10)
1. Mean
2. Confusing
3. Wasteful
4. **Beautiful**

5 What did Judas do after he took the thirty silver coins from the chief priests? (26:15-16)
1. **He watched for an opportunity to hand over Jesus to the chief priest.**
2. He ran away.
3. He went to the house of Simon the Leper.
4. He watched for a Roman soldier.

6 Whom did Jesus say that Judas would betray? (26:23-25)
1. John
2. Joseph
3. **Jesus**
4. Peter

7 While they ate the Passover meal, what did Jesus do with the bread? (26:26)
1. He gave thanks, and he broke the bread.
2. He gave the bread to his disciples.
3. He said, "Take and eat; this is my body."
4. **All of the above**

8 What did Jesus say when he took the cup, he gave thanks, and he offered it to them? (26:27-28)
1. "Drink from it, all of you."
2. "This is my blood of the covenant."
3. "This is poured out for many for the forgiveness of sins."
4. **All of the above**

9 During which holiday did Jesus give his disciples new meaning for the bread and cup? (26:19, 26-28)
1. The Bar Mitzphah
2. The Day of Atonement
3. **The Passover**
4. Hanukkah

10 Finish this verse: "In him we have redemption through his blood, . . ." (Ephesians 1:7)
1. ". . . and receive salvation by his grace."
2. ". . . we are his children, and he has saved us."
3. **". . . the forgiveness of sins, in accordance with the riches of God's grace."**
4. ". . . when we take Communion."

sixteen

Matthew 26:31-56

Memory Verse

"Going a little farther, he fell with his face to the ground and prayed, 'My Father, if it is possible, may this cup be taken from me. Yet not as I will, but as you will'" (Matthew 26:39).

Biblical Truth

Jesus struggled, but he chose to follow the will of God for our salvation.

Focus

This lesson will teach the children that even when struggles come, it is important to follow the will of God for us. God does not wish for anyone to suffer. However, suffering does occur as a result of the sinful choices of humanity.

Teaching Tip

As you lead the Bible study, remind the children that the will of God is more important than the will of people. Jesus knew this, and he reflected it in his prayer.

BIBLICAL COMMENTARY

It is true that Jesus planned to sacrifice himself to save humanity from the sin and the death. It is also true that he freely chose to go to Jerusalem to fulfil the prophecy of Old Testament prophets. He did not run away. Nevertheless, his imminent suffering and his death were not easy to bear.

When Jesus was "overwhelmed with sorrow to the point of death," he gave to us the greatest example of how to respond to suffering--he turned to the Father. Jesus honestly told the Father that he would prefer to avoid crucifixion. However, he submitted himself to the Father's will. Jesus knew the results of the suffering were greater than the suffering.

After this struggle, Jesus resolved to follow the will of God. The resolve of Jesus stands in sharp contrast to the resolve of the disciples. The disciples claimed that they would support Jesus. However, the disciples failed to watch, to pray, and to resist the temptation. The disciples also failed to remain loyal to Christ in the face of the danger. They did not seek their strength from God, and their own strength was insufficient.

Jesus was human as well as divine. Jesus knows our human limitations and the depths of suffering. Jesus shows us the right path to take. This path is to follow the guidance of God and to submit to the will of God regardless of the cost. Nothing is more valuable than to maintain our relationship with God through obedience.

CHARACTERISTICS OF GOD

- Jesus prayed for the will of God.
- Jesus chose to follow the will of God for our salvation.

WORDS OF OUR FAITH

The **will of God** is the redemption God wants for all of His creation. The Holy Spirit reveals the will of God to us as we pray, read the Bible, and talk with experienced Christians.

PEOPLE

The **sons of Zebedee** were James and John.
The **Son of Man** was a name for Jesus.

PLACES

Galilee was a northern area in Palestine where Jesus grew up and preached.
Gethsemane was a garden on the Mount of Olives.

THINGS

To **disown** means to reject, to deny, or to turn your back on someone.
This cup refers to the deep sorrow and the suffering that Jesus would soon endure.
To **betray** means to use the trust of a friend to harm that person.

A **legion** was a unit of 6,000 Roman soldiers. Twelve legions of angels would be 72,000 angels.

ACTIVITY

You will need these items for this activity:

- Some tape or a rope

Before class, create two parallel lines on the floor. The lines should be about 5 or 6 meters apart. Make lines long enough for all of the children to stand on them. Use the tape or the rope to mark the lines. These lines mark the beginning and the end of the walk that the children will take. Tell the children to divide into some groups of two. Offer the children some help if they need it.

Say, **Today, we will learn how God helps us when things are difficult. Each pair of children will send one person to the starting line. This is not a race. There will be no winner. All of you who are at the start must cross the finish. To get there, you must hop on one foot for the entire way. After we finish, we will repeat this activity. However, the second time you can put one hand on your partner, and your partner can guide you to the finish line.**

Wait until each child has passed the finish line. Say, **It was difficult to hop on one foot to the finish line. However, it was much easier when your partner could support you. Today we will learn how God helped Jesus when Jesus went through a difficult time.**

BIBLICAL LESSON

Prepare the following story, adapted from Matthew 26:31-56, before you tell it to the children.

Jesus said to his disciples, "Tonight, you will abandon me. However, after I rise from the dead, I will go ahead of you into Galilee."

Peter said, "Even if everyone else abandons you, I will never abandon you."

Jesus said, "Tonight, before the rooster crows, you will disown me three times."

Peter said, "Even if I must die with you, I will not disown you." The other disciples agreed with Peter.

Jesus went with his disciples to Gethsemane. Jesus said, "Stay here. I will go on and pray." He took Peter, James, and John with him. Jesus was extremely sorrowful and troubled. He said to his disciples, "My soul feels overwhelmed by sorrow. Please stay here, and pray for me."

Jesus went further into the garden, and he fell on his face to pray. He said, "Father, if it is possible, may this cup be taken from me. However, I want to do your will, not mine."

Jesus returned to his disciples. They were asleep. Jesus asked, "Could you not stay awake with me for one hour?"

He said to Peter, "Pray with all of your might. That way, you will not fall into temptation. The spirit is willing, but the flesh is weak."

Jesus returned to pray again. He said, "My Father, if it is not possible for this cup to be taken away unless I drink it, may your will be done."

When Jesus returned to his disciples, they were again asleep, because they were extremely tired. Jesus left them again, and he prayed a third time.

Then Jesus returned to his disciples. He said to them, "Are you still asleep? The time has come for the betrayer to give me to the sinners. We must go now. My betrayer comes!"

While Jesus spoke, Judas arrived with a large crowd. Previously, Judas arranged a signal with the crowd. Judas told them, "The one whom I kiss is the man. He is the one that you should arrest." Judas went immediately to Jesus, and he said, "Greetings, Rabbi!" Judas kissed Jesus.

Jesus said, "Friend, do what you came to do." Some men stepped forward, and they arrested Jesus. One of the disciples grabbed a sword, and he attacked the servant of the high priest. The disciple cut off the ear of the servant.

Jesus said, "Put your sword away. People who resort to violence will suffer death in a violent way. If I wanted to do it, I could call on my Father. He would send twelve legions of angels to defend me. However, this would not fulfil the Scripture."

Jesus said to the crowd, "I do not lead a rebellion. Why have you come with swords and clubs to capture me? I taught everyday in the Temple courts, but you did not arrest me then. However, this must happen to fulfil the writings of the prophets."

Then the disciples abandoned Jesus, and they fled away.

Encourage the children to answer the following questions. There are no right or wrong answers. These questions help the children to understand the story and to apply it to their lives.

1. How did Peter feel when Jesus said that Peter would disown Jesus? Have you ever defended a friend, even when others did not? Was it easy or difficult?
2. Jesus earnestly prayed that God would permit him not to die. Have you ever had to do something for God that you did not want to do? How did you feel about it?
3. Why did the disciples run away after the crowd arrested Jesus? How do you think Jesus felt about this? Have you ever had friends who did not defend you when you needed it? How did you feel?

Say, **What is God's will for me? This is a question that disturbs every Christian at some time in his or her life. Jesus was no exception. In the garden, Jesus was** extremely sad. He asked God if there was some other way to complete his mission. Then Jesus chose to do the will of God.

How do you find God's will? Read your Bible faithfully. Pray and listen for the direction from God. Seek the will of God in every area of your life. When you follow the will of God, you make the best decisions.

MEMORY VERSE

Practice the study's memory verse. You will find suggestions for Memory Verse Activities on pages 137-138.

ADDITIONAL ACTIVITIES

Choose from these options to enhance the children's Bible study.

1. As a class, talk about situations where prayer helped. Make a list of these situations. Ask those who spoke to share how God helped them in the situation.

2. Research the geography of Jerusalem in the day of Jesus. Draw a simple map to aid your discussion. Keep this map, and use it as the class discusses the crucifixion and the resurrection of Jesus.

QUESTIONS FOR BASIC COMPETITION

To prepare the children for competition, read Matthew 26:31-56 to them.

1 Where did Jesus say he would go after he had risen? (26:32)
   1. **Galilee**
   2. Rome
   3. Jerusalem

2 Who said "Even if I have to die with you, I will never disown you"? (26:35)
   1. Judas
   2. John
   3. **Peter**

3 Whom did Jesus take aside with him when he went to pray in Gethsemane? (26:37)
   1. Mark, John, and Judas
   2. **Peter and the two sons of Zebedee**
   3. Peter and Judas

4 How did Jesus feel when he went to pray in Gethsemane? (26:37)
   1. Sorrowful
   2. Troubled
   3. **Both answers are correct.**

5 What did Jesus do when he started to pray in Gethsemane? (26:39)
   1. **He fell with his face to the ground.**
   2. He sat on a rock.
   3. He stood.

6 What did Jesus pray for God to do when he prayed in Gethsemane? (26:39)
   1. "May this cup be taken from me."
   2. "Yet not as I will, but as you will."
   3. **Both answers are correct.**

7 What did Jesus ask Peter when he found the disciples asleep? (26:40)
   1. "Why did you disappoint me?"
   2. **"Could you men not keep watch with me for one hour?"**
   3. "Have you seen Judas?"

8 What was the signal that Judas gave for the arrest of Jesus? (26:48)
   1. A handshake
   2. **A kiss**
   3. A hug

9 What happened when the men stepped forward, seized Jesus, and arrested him? (26:50-51)
   1. **One of the companions of Jesus cut off the ear of the servant of the high priest.**
   2. The men dropped dead.
   3. Both answers are correct.

10 After the arrest of Jesus, what did the disciples do? (26:56)
   1. They continued to sleep.
   2. They stayed with him until the end.
   3. **They left him, and they ran away.**

QUESTIONS FOR ADVANCED COMPETITION

To prepare the children for competition, read Matthew 26:31-56 to them.

1 What did Jesus say would happen three times before the rooster crowed? (26:34)
1. The Pharisees would arrest Jesus.
2. The crowd would crucify Jesus.
3. God would raise Jesus from the dead.
4. **Peter would deny Jesus.**

2 Why did Jesus go to Gethsemane? (26:36)
1. To fast
2. **To pray**
3. To be alone
4. To celebrate the Passover

3 What did Jesus say to Peter, James, and John when he prayed in the Garden of Gethsemane? (26:37-38)
1. "Leave me in peace until I come to you."
2. "Stay here and rest a while."
3. **"Stay here and keep watch with me."**
4. "Go to the entrance and keep watch."

4 What did Jesus pray the first time in Gethsemane? (26:39)
1. **"My Father, if it is possible, may this cup be taken from me. Yet not as I will, but as you will."**
2. "I am ready to die."
3. "Father, please send angels to help me."
4. "Please help my disciples."

5 When Jesus returned to his disciples, what did he find? (26:40)
1. A band of robbers were there.
2. **His disciples were asleep.**
3. A meal, prepared by his disciples, was ready.
4. A venomous snake was there.

6 How long did Jesus pray before he found his disciples asleep for the first time? (26:40)
1. **One hour**
2. Twenty minutes
3. Two hours
4. Ten minutes

7 When the soldiers came to arrest Jesus, what did Jesus say? (26:45)
1. "The Son of Man is betrayed into the fingers of liars."
2. "The Son of Man is betrayed into the arms of lions."
3. "The Son of Man is betrayed into the mouth of snakes."
4. **"The Son of Man is betrayed into the hands of sinners."**

8 What did Judas do to Jesus in Gethsemane? (26:47-49)
1. He prayed with Jesus.
2. **He betrayed Jesus.**
3. He embraced Jesus.
4. He slapped Jesus.

9 What did the men who came with Judas do when Judas kissed Jesus? (26:50)
1. They tried to kill the disciples.
2. They fell to the ground in fear.
3. **They seized Jesus, and they arrested him.**
4. They ran away.

10 Finish this verse: "Going a little farther, he fell with his face to the ground and prayed, 'My Father, if it is possible...'" (Matthew 26:39)
1. "...let me live so that I may see your glory on the earth.'"
2. "...may the sun not rise until I glorify your name.'"
3. **"...may this cup be taken from me. Yet not as I will, but as you will."**
4. "...forgive the sins of these people.'"

seventeen

Matthew 26:57--27:5

Memory Verse

"Then Jesus said to his disciples, 'If anyone would come after me, he must deny himself and take up his cross and follow me'" (Matthew 16:24).

Biblical Truth

Jesus remained faithful to his Father though others were against him.

Focus

In this lesson, children will learn that when others betrayed, denied, or lied about Jesus, he was faithful to fulfil the will of God for our salvation.

Teaching Tip

Review key terms from other studies. Some important terms you may need to refer to are: Caiaphas, high priest, and Son of Man.

BIBLICAL COMMENTARY

In this lesson, we see a sharp contrast. Jesus was faithful to God in all things. Some people who should act faithfully were not faithful. The worst offenders were the chief priests and the Sanhedrin. The chief priests represented the people to God, and they represented God to the people.

The Sanhedrin contained the priests, the Pharisees, the Sadducees, and certain family elders. The Romans gave the Sanhedrin the authority to rule over Jewish civil issues. The members of the Sanhedrin were the guardians of the godliness and the justice. Instead, the Sanhedrin did whatever they could to condemn Jesus. Under the pretence of honour to God, they revealed themselves as the enemies of Jesus.

A person would expect Judas, as one of the disciples, to show a trustworthy nature. Instead, he participated in the wickedness of the chief priests. Judas eventually felt remorse, but he did not repent and turn to God for forgiveness. Instead, he killed himself in despair.

We expect Peter and Judas to show a faithful nature. However, Peter lied as soon as he felt threatened. Unlike Judas, Peter repented for his unfaithfulness.

CHARACTERISTICS OF GOD

- Jesus followed the will of God even when others did not.
- Jesus remained faithful to God.

WORDS OF OUR FAITH

To be faithful is to show dependability and trustworthiness. God is always **faithful**. We can trust him to keep his promises. God expects his people to show **faithfulness** to him and to others.

PEOPLE

The **Sanhedrin** was the supreme court and the law-making branch for the Jews. The Sanhedrin contained 71 members—the chief priests, the elders, and the teachers of the Law. The high priest was the leader of this group.

The **Mighty One** is another name for God.

Chief Priests were the priests who served in higher ranks in the Temple. They were a part of the Sanhedrin.

PLACES

The **Temple of God** was the Temple in Jerusalem.

OTHER TERMS

Blasphemy is any word or action that a person uses to curse God, to show disrespect for God, or to claim the person is God.

ACTIVITY

You will need these items for this activity:
- Various craft items to make a cross (beads, leather, nails, clay, wood)

Provide the supplies that you have to help each child to make a small cross. Show a sample cross to the children. Demonstrate the steps to make a cross. If possible, encourage the children to write the memory verse on the cross after the children complete the cross.

BIBLICAL LESSON

Prepare the following story, adapted from Matthew 26:57--27:5 before you tell it to the children.

The people who arrested Jesus took him to Caiaphas, the high priest. Peter followed this group to the courtyard to observe the outcome. The chief priests and the Sanhedrin looked for false evidence against Jesus because they wanted to kill him. Many false witnesses testified, but there was no evidence. Finally two people came forward.

They said, "This man said, 'I am able to destroy the Temple of God and rebuild it in three days.'"

The high priest asked Jesus to respond, but Jesus kept silent.

The high priest said, "Tell us if you are the Christ, the Son of God."

Jesus said, "Yes, it is as you say. In the future you will see the Son of Man as he sits at the right hand of the Mighty One."

The high priest tore his clothes, and he said, "He spoke blasphemy!"

The people yelled, "He is worthy of death." Then they spit in the face of Jesus, and they struck him with their fists. Then they ridiculed him and said, "Prophesy to us, Christ. Who hit you?"

Peter was in the courtyard when a servant girl said, "You also were with Jesus of Galilee."

Peter denied it. "I do not know what you talk about," he said.

When Peter left the courtyard, another girl said, "This fellow was with Jesus of Nazareth."

Peter denied it again, with an oath. He said, "I do not know the man!"

Other people came to Peter and they said, "Surely you are one of them, for your accent indicates this."

Peter swore to them, "I do not know the man!"

Immediately a rooster crowed. Peter remembered the words of Jesus, "Before the rooster crows, you will disown me three times."

Peter went outside, and he wept bitterly.

Early in the morning, all of the chief priests and the elders of the people came to the decision to put to death Jesus. They bound him, and they took him to Pilate, the governor.

Judas felt guilty. He returned the thirty silver coins to the chief priests and the elders.

"I handed over an innocent man," he said. "What is that to us?" they replied.

So Judas threw the money into the Temple, and he left. Then Judas went away, and he hanged himself.

Encourage the children to answer the following questions. There are no right or wrong answers. These questions will help the children to understand the story and to apply it to their lives.

1. Why did the Sanhedrin want false evidence against Jesus? What kind of false evidence do you think they wanted?
2. Did Caiaphas believe that Jesus was the Son of God? Explain your answer.
3. Why did the Sanhedrin decide to put to death Jesus?
4. What do you think Peter thought when he disowned Jesus? How do you think he felt after he disowned Jesus?
5. What feelings do you think Judas felt before, during, and after he betrayed Jesus?

Say, **Good friends are valuable. Everyone needs some good friends. A really good friend will stand by you when everyone else deserts you. Do you have a dependable friend to help you?**

Jesus had some good friends, his disciples. Jesus spent much time with Peter, James, and John. Yet, when Jesus faced a trial, his friends left him. One even denied three times that he knew Jesus.

Our friends may disappoint us. However, Jesus is our friend forever. You can trust Jesus. Jesus stayed faithful to God, and he will remain faithful to you.

MEMORY VERSE

Practice the study's memory verse. You will find suggestions for Memory Verse Activities on pages 137-138.

ADDITIONAL ACTIVITIES

Choose from any of these options to enhance the children's Bible study.

1. Research the judicial system of your government. What happens during a trial? How does the judge consider evidence? How does your system differ from the trial of Jesus with the Sanhedrin?

2. Compare and contrast the lives of Peter and Judas. Read the stories in Matthew that relate to each man. What character traits did each person display throughout his life? What is similar about their actions in the story for today? How did each person deal with his guilt? Make a poster that displays your findings. Read ahead in Acts to find out more about Peter.

QUESTIONS FOR BASIC COMPETITION

To prepare the children for competition, read Matthew 26:57--27:5 to them.

1 Where did the people take Jesus after his arrest? (26:57)
1. To Herod
2. To Peter
3. To Caiaphas

2 Who followed at a distance after the arrest of Jesus? (26:57-58)
1. John
2. Peter
3. Paul

3 For what did the chief priests and the Sanhedrin look during the trial of Jesus? (26:59)
1. True witnesses to accuse Jesus
2. Real evidence against Jesus
3. False evidence against Jesus

4 The high priest asked Jesus to tell the people if he was the Christ. What did Jesus say? (26:63-64)
1. "Yes, it is as you say."
2. "I am not the Christ."
3. "Ask the people."

5 What did the people do after the high priest said that Jesus spoke blasphemy? (26:65, 67)
1. They shook the hand of Jesus.
2. They spit on Jesus, and they hit him.
3. They guarded Jesus to protect him.

6 What clue told the people that Peter was a follower of Jesus? (26:73)
1. His hair
2. His accent
3. His clothing

7 What happened after Peter denied Jesus three times? (26:69-74)
1. A rooster crowed.
2. James and John reminded Peter of the words of Jesus.
3. A soldier arrested Peter.

8 What did the chief priests and the elders decide to do to Jesus after his trial? (27:1)
1. To release Jesus
2. To put Jesus to death
3. To put Jesus in prison

9 Who said "I have sinned, . . . for I have betrayed innocent blood"? (27:4)
1. Caiaphas
2. Peter
3. Judas

10 What did Judas do with the money that he received for his betrayal of Jesus? (27:5)
1. He threw it in a well.
2. He gave it to the poor.
3. He threw it in the Temple.

QUESTIONS FOR ADVANCED COMPETITION

To prepare the children for competition, read Matthew 26:57--27:5 to them.

1 For what did the chief priests and the Sanhedrin look during the trial of Jesus? (26:59)
1. The truth about Jesus
2. The proof that Jesus was the true Messiah
3. False evidence so that they could put Jesus to death
4. All of the above

2 After the false testimony during the trial of Jesus, how did Jesus react? (26:60-63)
1. He defended himself.
2. He looked confused.
3. He remained silent.
4. He tried to escape.

3 What did Jesus say when Caiaphas asked him if he was the Christ, the Son of God? (26:63-64)
1. "Yes, it is as you say."
2. "I am not."
3. "Ask the people."
4. All of the above

4 What did Jesus say that the Sanhedrin would see in the future? (26:64)
1. "The Son of Man sitting at the right hand of the Mighty One and coming on the clouds of heaven"
2. "The glory of God"
3. "The Messiah coming forth from the grave"
4. "A new heaven and a new earth"

5 What did the high priest do when he said that Jesus spoke blasphemy? (26:65)
1. He fell to his knees and prayed that God would forgive Jesus.
2. He hit Jesus.
3. He tore his clothes.
4. He ran from the room.

6 What did the servant girl tell to Peter when he sat in the courtyard? (26:69)
1. He was with Jesus of Galilee.
2. He was the man who betrayed Jesus.
3. He will experience an arrest, too.
4. All of the above

7 How did Peter respond to the second person who told him that he was a follower of Jesus? (26:71-72)
1. "I don't know the man!"
2. "I was his friend, but I am not his friend now."
3. "I am proud to say that Jesus is my friend."
4. All of the above

8 What did Peter do when he remembered that Jesus said that Peter would disown him three times? (26:75)
1. He went outside, and he wept bitterly.
2. He ran, and he asked Jesus to forgive him.
3. He ran away, and he hid in the Temple.
4. All of the above

9 What did Judas do when the chief priests and the elders did not take back the money? (27:5)
1. He hanged himself.
2. He tried to help Jesus to escape.
3. He ran away, and he hid in Nazareth.
4. He asked Jesus for forgiveness.

10 Finish this verse: "Then Jesus said to his disciples, 'If anyone would come after me, he must deny himself and . . .'" (Matthew 16:24)
1. "'. . . take up his staff and follow me.'"
2. "'. . . take up his cross and follow me.'"
3. "'. . . take up his robes and follow me.'"
4. "'. . . take up his mat and follow me.'"

eighteen

Matthew 27:11-31

Memory Verse

"'What shall I do, then, with Jesus who is called Christ?'" (Matthew 27:22a)

Biblical Truth

Jesus gives to people a choice about how they will respond to him.

Focus

This lesson will help the children learn that they will choose how they will respond to Jesus.

Teaching Tip

As you lead the Bible study, focus on the ways that different people responded to Jesus. Focus especially on Pilate and the role that Pilate played in the death of Jesus.

BIBLICAL COMMENTARY

This lesson gives us the opportunity to see how different people chose to respond to Jesus. Pilate, the Roman governor, had the opportunity to choose if he would support Jesus. Since Jews had to follow Roman law, they did not have the authority to give the death penalty. They needed the permission of Pilate for this to happen.

Pilate thought that Jesus was innocent by the standards of Roman law. Pilate saw how much the Jewish leaders were envious of the popularity and the leadership of Jesus. Pilate had to choose if he would convict Jesus to death, or if he would deal with a Jewish revolt against him. Pilate chose to avoid the responsibility, and he allowed Jesus to die.

Additionally, the crowd had a choice about how they would respond to Jesus. Pilate gave them a choice between two prisoners, Jesus or Barabbas. The crowd thought that Jesus would be a strong political leader. When Jesus did not meet this expectation, the crowd asked for the release of Barabbas. They wanted the Romans to crucify Jesus.

CHARACTERISTICS OF GOD

- Jesus did not fight back when others wronged him.
- Jesus wants us to choose to follow him.

WORDS OF OUR FAITH

Choices are decisions about what to do. We make right **choices** when we obey God. We make wrong **choices** when we disobey God.

PEOPLE

Barabbas was a man who was in prison for murder and rioting.

Pilate was the Roman governor over Judea and Samaria. It was his responsibility to keep the peace among the Jews.

THINGS

To **flog** means to beat a person with a whip or rod.

To **crucify** means to attach a person to a cross as a punishment.

The **Praetorium** was the headquarters of the Roman governor.

ACTIVITY

You will need these items for this activity:

- Chalk, dry-erase markers, or a pen
- A chalkboard, a whiteboard, or a large piece of paper

Before class begins, write the following sentences and post them where the children can read them.

Who is Jesus?

He is the Son of God.

What did Jesus do for you?

He died for our sins.

What shall you "'do, then, with Jesus who is called Christ?'"

I will receive him as my Saviour.

How will you help others know Jesus?

I will tell them about Jesus and what he did to save the people from their sins.

If others refuse to follow Jesus, what will you do?

I will continue to follow Jesus.

Say, **I wrote some sentences that I want us to read together. I will read the questions, then you will read the answers.**

Say, **Jesus gives to us a choice to follow him or not to follow him. He wants us to follow him, but he does not force us to follow him.** If it is appropriate, ask if any child wants to ask Jesus to become their Saviour and best Friend. Close in prayer, and ask God to help every student to choose to follow Jesus.

BIBLICAL LESSON

Prepare the following story, adapted from Matthew 27:11-31, before you tell it to the children.

Jesus went to the governor, Pontius Pilate. The governor asked Jesus, "Are you the king of the Jews?"

Jesus replied, "Yes, it is as you say."

The chief priests and the elders gave many accusations against Jesus. However, Jesus did not respond to them. Pilate was surprised that Jesus did not make a response.

Every year, during the feast of Passover, Pilate released a prisoner whom the crowd chose. At this time, there was a prisoner with the name of Barrabas. Pilate asked the crowd, "Whom should I release this year--Jesus or Barrabas?"

Earlier in that day, Pilate received a message from his wife about Jesus. The

message said, "Do not have anything to do with that innocent man. I had a dream about him last night, and the dream caused me to suffer." However, the chief priests said that they wanted Pilate to release Barrabas instead of Jesus.

Again, Pilate asked, "Which man should I release to you?" Again, the crowd demanded that Pilate release Barrabas. Pilate asked, "What should I do with Jesus?"

The crowd answered, "Crucify him!"

Pilate said, "Why should I crucify him? What crime did he commit?"

However, the crowd shouted louder, "Crucify him!"

Pilate noticed the agitation of the crowd. Pilate knew that a riot could happen. Because of this, Pilate brought a basin of water, and he washed his hands. He said, "I am innocent of the blood of this man. It is your responsibility."

The crowd said, "Let his blood be on us and on our children!" Then Pilate released Barrabas. Pilate ordered that the soldiers flog Jesus. Pilate gave Jesus to the crowd so that they could crucify him.

The soldiers took Jesus to the Praetorium. They took off his outer clothes, and then they put a scarlet robe on him. They made a crown from some thorns, and they put the crown on his head. They also gave Jesus a staff. Then they knelt in front of Jesus, and they mocked him. The soldiers said, "Hail, king of the Jews!" They spit on Jesus, and they beat him repeatedly on the head. After the soldiers mocked Jesus, they put his clothes back on him. Then the soldiers took Jesus to crucify him.

Encourage the children to answer the following questions. There are no right or wrong answers. These questions help the children to understand the story and to apply it to their lives.

1. Why do you think that Jesus did not respond to the charges against him?

2. Why do you think Pilate did not respond to the concerns of his wife? Have you ever given some advice to a friend that your friend did not follow?

3. Pilate washed his hands, and he said that he was innocent of the death of Jesus. Do you think that Pilate was truly innocent? Who do you think had the biggest share of responsibility for the death of Jesus?

Say, We make choices every day of our lives. Some of our choices have little impact on our lives. Other choices can change our lives in major ways. The crowd and Pilate had a choice to make. They made the choice to crucify Jesus. Their choice changed the course of our history.

Today people face the same question, "How will you respond to Jesus?" Your response to that question will change the course of your life. How have you answered that question? What choice have you made?

MEMORY VERSE

Practice the study's memory verse. You will find suggestions for Memory Verse Activities on pages 137-138.

ADDITIONAL ACTIVITIES

Choose from these options to enhance the children's Bible study.

1. Ask the children to imagine that they are a character in today's study. How would they respond during the trial of Jesus? What would be different about their responses?

2. As a class, discuss who holds the most blame for the death of Jesus. Hold a trial, and look at the evidence for and against each character in the story.

QUESTIONS FOR BASIC COMPETITION

To prepare the children for competition, read Matthew Matthew 27:11-31 to them.

1 What did Jesus say when Pilate asked, "Are you the king of the Jews?" (27:11)
1. "No."
2. **"Yes, it is as you say."**
3. "Why do you want to know?"

2 How did Pilate feel when Jesus did not reply to a single charge? (27:14)
1. He was satisfied.
2. He was sad.
3. **He was amazed.**

3 What custom did the governor have at the feast? (27:15)
1. **He released a prisoner.**
2. He put someone in jail.
3. He crucified someone.

4 What choice did Pilate give to the people about Barabbas and Jesus? (27:17)
1. To keep both in prison
2. **To release Jesus or Barabbas**
3. To crucify both of them

5 Who told Pilate to have nothing to do with Jesus? (27:19)
1. **The wife of Pilate**
2. An angel of the Lord
3. Mary, the mother of Jesus

6 Who persuaded the crowd to ask for the release of Barabbas? (27:20)
1. Judas
2. **The chief priests and the elders**
3. The disciples of Jesus

7 What did the crowd tell Pilate to do with Jesus? (27:22)
1. "Release him!"
2. "Stone him!"
3. **"Crucify him!"**

8 Who said "Let his blood be on us and on our children!"? (27:25)
1. The chief priests and elders
2. Pilate and Herod
3. **The crowd who condemned Jesus**

9 What colour was the robe that the soldiers placed on Jesus? (27:28)
1. Navy
2. **Scarlet**
3. White

10 What did the soldiers do before they took Jesus for the crucifixion? (27:30-31)
1. **They spit on him, and they struck him on the head.**
2. They stepped on him.
3. They dragged him around Jerusalem.

QUESTIONS FOR ADVANCED COMPETITION

To prepare the children for competition, read Matthew 27:11-31 to them.

1 How did Jesus answer Pilate's question, "Are you the king of the Jews"? (27:11)
1. Jesus said nothing.
2. **Jesus said, "Yes, it is as you say."**
3. Jesus said, "The Son of Man has come to shed his blood for the forgiveness of many."
4. Jesus quoted Isaiah 53.

2 Why did Pilate allow the crowd to select a prisoner to be released? (27:15)
1. **It was the custom of the governor at the feast.**
2. He was afraid of the high priest.
3. He did not have the authority to release Jesus.
4. All of the above

3 Who was Barabbas? (27:16)
1. A notorious politician
2. The brother of Jesus
3. A disciple
4. **A notorious prisoner**

4 What did the people at the trial do because of envy? (27:18)
1. **They handed over Jesus to Pilate.**
2. They shouted at each other.
3. They handed over Jesus to Herod.
4. They listened to Jesus.

5 What did the wife of Pilate tell him during the trial of Jesus? (27:19)
1. "I would like you to crucify Jesus."
2. **"I have suffered a great deal today in a dream because of him."**
3. "Let me know what you decide to do."
4. "You should release Barabbas."

6 Why did the crowd start an uproar? (27:24)
1. Jesus started to get angry.
2. **Pilate tried to defend Jesus.**
3. Barabbas started to get violent.
4. Pilate started to send some people to the Temple.

7 What did the crowd say about the responsibility for the death of Jesus? (27:25)
1. **"Let his blood be on us and on our children!"**
2. "It is your responsibility."
3. "His blood will be on the Pharisees and the Sadducees."
4. "It was Judas who sold Jesus for 30 pieces of silver. Let the blood of Jesus stay on Judas."

8 After he washed his hands, what did Pilate do? (27:26)
1. He released Barabbas.
2. He flogged Jesus.
3. He handed over Jesus for crucifixion.
4. **All of the above**

9 What three items did the soldiers make Jesus use before his crucifixion? (27:28-29)
1. A robe, a crown of thorns, and a pair of sandals
2. A robe, a sceptre, and some wine
3. **A robe, a crown of thorns, and a staff**
4. A crown of thorns, some wine, and a sceptre

10 Finish this verse: "What shall I do, then, with..." (27:22a)
1. "...Judas the betrayer?"
2. **"...Jesus who is called Christ?"**
3. "...Jesus who is called the Son of Man?"
4. "...Barrabas, the criminal?"

nineteen

Matthew 27:32-56

Memory Verse

"For God so loved the world that he gave his one and only Son, that whoever believes in him shall not perish but have eternal life" (John 3:16).

Biblical Truth

Jesus willingly suffered and died so that everyone, even his enemies, could receive salvation from sin.

Focus

In this lesson, children will learn that Jesus died on a cross for the forgiveness of our sins.

Teaching Tip

The passage in Matthew about the crucifixion of Jesus is less graphic than the version of the other Gospel writers. However, this lesson could traumatize some children. If any child asks for details about the crucifixion of Jesus, be sensitive to children who may not handle well the gruesome details of his death.

BIBLICAL COMMENTARY

While Jesus was on the Cross, he endured rejection from Jews and Gentiles (non-Jews). The Jews rejected him because he claimed to be the Son of God. The Gentiles rejected him because he claimed to be a king.

After the death of Jesus, many supernatural events happened. The Temple curtain tore from the top to the bottom. This event signified that believers could now communicate directly with God. An earthquake occurred, some graves opened up, and holy people became alive again.

These events amazed a Roman centurion and the guards with him. They recognized Jesus as the Son of God. Therefore, it was not a Jew who recognized the divinity of Jesus. Rather, it was a Roman guard, a Gentile.

These miraculous events signified the true identity of Jesus. They were the completion of his mission of atonement. This atonement is available through the death of Jesus on the Cross. The victory of Jesus on the Cross was his triumph over the sin of humanity.

On the Cross, Jesus felt the weight of the sin of the world on his shoulders. Despite the agony that Jesus endured, he chose to die so that everyone could receive forgiveness for sin.

CHARACTERISTICS OF GOD

- God loves us so much that he sent his son to show us how we can have abundant life.

123

- Jesus gave his life freely to demonstrate to us the love of the Father.

WORDS OF OUR FAITH

Salvation is everything that God does to take away sins and to create a right relationship between himself and a person. God sent his Son, Jesus, who died on the Cross and became our Saviour. Those who ask Jesus to be their Saviour receive **salvation** as a free gift.

PEOPLE

Mary Magdalene was a lady from the town of Magdala, on the Sea of Galilee.
Simon from Cyrene was the man who carried a cross for Jesus.

PLACES

Cyrene was a city in North Africa.
Golgotha was the place where Jesus died on the Cross.
The **holy city** is another name for Jerusalem.

OTHER TERMS

Gall is an extract from a plant. Jesus refused to drink a mixture of gall and wine when he was on the cross. The mixture would relieve pain.
The **Temple curtain** was a blue, purple, and scarlet curtain that separated the holy of holies from the outer rooms of the Temple.

ACTIVITY

You will need these items for this activity:
- Sheets of wood, poster board, or paper for each child
- Supplies needed to write, draw, and paint

Say, **Today we will learn about the death of Jesus on the Cross. The soldiers posted a written charge above the head of Jesus. The words were, "This is Jesus, the King of the Jews."**

What words would someone use to describe you?

Encourage the children to make a sign with only a few words to describe themselves. If possible, let the students frame the sign and take it home.

BIBLICAL LESSON

Prepare the following story, adapted from Matthew 27:32-56 before you tell it to the children.

As the soldiers went to Golgotha, they met Simon from Cyrene, and they forced him to carry a cross for Jesus.

They came to Golgotha. Golgotha means The Place of the Skull. There, the soldiers offered Jesus a mixture of gall and wine to drink. After Jesus tasted it, he refused to drink it.

When the soldiers crucified Jesus, they divided his clothes by the casting of the lots. Then the soldiers sat down to keep the watch. Above the head of Jesus

the soldiers placed the written charge against him that said, "THIS IS JESUS, THE KING OF THE JEWS."

Two robbers were on crosses with Jesus. One robber was on his right side, and one robber was on his left side. The people who passed by insulted him. They said, "Save yourself! Come down from the cross, if you are the Son of God!"

The chief priests, the teachers of the Law, and the elders mocked Jesus. They said, "He saved others, but he cannot save himself! Let him come down now from the cross, and we will believe in him. He trusts in God; let God rescue him now if he wants him, for he said, 'I am the Son of God.'"

The robbers who were next to him also insulted him.

From the sixth hour until the ninth hour, darkness came over all of the land. At about the ninth hour, Jesus cried out in a loud voice, "Eloi, Eloi, lama sabachthani?"--which means, "My God, my God, why have you forsaken me?"

Some people thought that Jesus called to Elijah. One person filled a sponge with wine vinegar, put it on a stick, and offered it to Jesus to drink.

Everyone else said, "Now leave him alone. Let us see if Elijah comes to save him."

Then, Jesus cried out in a loud voice, and he died.

At that moment, the curtain of the Temple tore in two pieces from top to bottom. The earth shook, and the rocks split. The tombs broke open, and the bodies of many holy people who died were alive again. These people went into the holy city, and they appeared to many people.

The centurion and those who guarded Jesus became afraid. They exclaimed, "Surely he was the Son of God!"

Many women followed Jesus from Galilee to care for his needs. Among them were Mary Magdalene, Mary the mother of James and Joses, and the mother of the sons of Zebedee. They watched all of these events from a distance.

Encourage the children to answer the following questions. There are no right or wrong answers. These questions will help the children to understand the story and to apply it to their lives.

1. Imagine that you were Simon of Cyrene. How do you think he felt when he carried a heavy cross for Jesus? Where were the disciples of Jesus? Do you think they should carry the cross for Jesus?

2. Imagine that you were a person in the crowd at the crucifixion of Jesus. How would you respond to him? Would you make fun of him?

3. Read Matthew 27:46. What kind of pain caused Jesus to say these words?

4. How do you think the centurion and the guards felt after the death of Jesus? How do you think the

chief priests and the elders felt? Do you think they finally believed that Jesus is God's Son?

5. What kinds of things do you think the women who took care of Jesus did for him? How do you think Jesus felt toward these women?

Say, **Jesus knew that God would allow him to suffer and die so that people could receive salvation. Jesus willingly gave his life for all people. Through the death of Jesus, we can receive forgiveness of sins and eternal life.**

Did you ask for forgiveness of your sins and accept Jesus as your Saviour yet? If you did this, you can rejoice with Jesus. If you did not do this, you can do it now. Jesus wants to welcome you as a member of the family of God.

MEMORY VERSE

Practice the study's memory verse. You will find suggestions for Memory Verse Activities on pages 137-138.

ADDITIONAL ACTIVITIES

Choose from any of these options to enhance the children's Bible study.

1. Encourage the children to think of something that they would sacrifice for someone else. An example is to sacrifice some time to help a brother or a sister with a chore or a job in the house. Or, you could sacrifice time or money to help a needy person. Ask, **What do you possess that you can sacrifice? How could your sacrifice help someone else?**

The sacrifice of Jesus was far greater than anything we can do. However, our sacrifice can help us sense how he felt when he gave his life to save people from their sins.

2. There were many different types of people who witnessed the death of Jesus. Read the story aloud to the children. As a group, write how each of the following groups acted: the crowd, the chief priests, the centurion and the soldiers, and the women. Ask, **What group would you join? How would you respond to Jesus?**

QUESTIONS FOR BASIC COMPETITION

To prepare the children for competition, read Matthew Matthew 27:11-31 to them.

1 Who carried a cross for Jesus? (27:32)
1. Judas from Samaria
2. Mary from Magdala
3. Simon from Cyrene

2 Where did they take Jesus to crucify him? (27:33)
1. Galilee
2. Golgotha
3. The Dead Sea

3 What did the soldiers do with the clothes of Jesus? (27:35)
1. They divided his clothes by the casting of the lots.
2. They sold them.
3. They gave them to the poor.

4 When Jesus was on the Cross, what did the sign above him say? (27:37)
1. "This is Jesus, the traitor."
2. "This is Jesus, the King of the Jews."
3. "This is the man they call Jesus."

5 Who was on the crosses next to Jesus? (27:38)
1. Barabbas and Judas
2. Two robbers
3. Peter and John

6 What did the two robbers next to Jesus do? (27:44)
1. They heaped insults on Jesus.
2. They begged Jesus to forgive them.
3. Both answers are correct.

7 What did the people try to give to Jesus when they thought that he called to Elijah? (27:47-48)
1. Water
2. Wine vinegar
3. Both answers are correct.

8 When Jesus died, what happened to the Temple? (27:50-51)
1. A fire destroyed the Temple.
2. The Temple curtain tore from top to bottom.
3. The temple collapsed.

9 What did the holy people who came out of the tombs do? (27:52-53)
1. They appeared to many people in the holy city.
2. They healed the sick.
3. They preached the gospel.

10 When did the centurion and those who guarded Jesus say that Jesus is the Son of God? (27:54)
1. When Jesus did not fight back
2. When they saw all that happened
3. Both answers are correct.

QUESTIONS FOR ADVANCED COMPETITION

To prepare the children for competition, read Matthew 27:11-31 to them.

1 What did Simon from Cyrene do? (27:32)
   1. He carried a cross for Jesus.
   2. He flogged Jesus.
   3. He nailed the hands of Jesus to the cross.
   4. He mocked Jesus.

2 What does *Golgotha* mean? (27:33)
   1. The Place of the Death
   2. The Place of the Skull
   3. The Field of the Blood
   4. The Field of the Potter

3 What did the people do when they walked by Jesus on the Cross? (27:39-40)
   1. They insulted Jesus.
   2. They prayed to Jesus.
   3. They asked Jesus for mercy.
   4. All of the above

4 What did the people tell Jesus to do, if he was the Son of God? (27:40)
   1. To part the Red Sea
   2. To come down from the Cross
   3. To kill the Roman soldiers
   4. To kill the chief priest

5 What did Jesus cry out? (27:46)
   1. "I am sorry."
   2. "Come, Elijah, and save me."
   3. "My God, my God, why have you forsaken me?"
   4. "The day of judgment is upon you."

6 Why did some people say, "Leave him alone," when Jesus cried out on the Cross? (27:49)
   1. They wanted to see if God would send some angels to rescue Jesus.
   2. They wanted Jesus to suffer.
   3. They thought an evil spirit possessed Jesus.
   4. They wanted to see if Elijah would come to save him.

7 What happened before Jesus gave up his spirit and died? (27:50)
   1. Jesus cried out in a loud voice.
   2. Jesus ate bread, and he drank juice.
   3. Jesus prayed the Lord's Prayer.
   4. Jesus caused an earthquake.

8 Who was terrified and said, "Surely he was the Son of God"? (27:54)
   1. The chief priests
   2. The Pharisees
   3. The centurion and those who guarded Jesus
   4. The disciples

9 Who were three of the women who followed Jesus from Galilee to care for his needs? (27:55-56)
   1. Mary, Martha, Tabitha
   2. Mary Magdalene, Mary the mother of James and Joses, and the mother of James and John
   3. Martha, Mary, Dorcas
   4. Three women named Mary

10 Finish this verse: "For God so loved the world that he gave his one and only Son, that whoever . . ." (John 3:16)
   1. ". . . knows him, knows God."
   2. ". . . believes in him shall not perish but have eternal life."
   3. ". . . shares his love, will receive love."
   4. ". . . asks him for forgiveness will receive it."

twenty

Matthew 27:57--28:20

Memory Verse

"'Therefore go and make disciples of all nations, baptizing them in the name of the Father and of the Son and of the Holy Spirit, and teaching them to obey everything I have commanded you. And surely I am with you always, to the very end of the age'" (Matthew 28:19-20).

Biblical Truth

Jesus rose from the dead, and he told to his followers the Great Commission.

Focus

In this lesson, the children will learn that Jesus commanded his followers to make disciples of all people.

Teaching Tip

As you lead the Bible study, focus on the miracle of the Resurrection. Because Jesus is alive, we have hope for a changed life.

BIBLICAL COMMENTARY

Joseph of Arimathea was a member of the Sanhedrin, the council that condemned Jesus. According to Mark and Luke, Joseph was a secret disciple of Christ.

It was not unusual for someone to bury his master. When Joseph asked Pilate for the body of Jesus, this was not unusual. Under Roman law, when criminals died, they would not receive a proper burial. When Joseph spent his time and money to give Jesus a proper burial, he honoured Jesus.

This situation provided evidence for the resurrection in three ways. First, the fact that the body of Jesus was in a new tomb with a stone that covered the entrance meant that Jesus was dead. Second, the stone would not allow any human to leave the tomb. Finally, a person could not substitute another body for the body of Jesus.

The chief priests and Pharisees remembered the prophecy of Jesus that he would rise after three days. They made arrangements to prevent the disciples from a declaration that a resurrection happened. However, the earthquake, the angel, the fearful guards, and the rolled-away stone were additional evidences of the resurrection of Jesus.

This evidence proved that Jesus was who he claimed to be and that his mission was successful. The atonement of Jesus was complete in the Resurrection. Believers can now experience new life because of the death and the resurrection of Jesus.

CHARACTERISTICS OF GOD

- Jesus rose from the dead, and he proved his power over death.
- Jesus wants us to make disciples of all nations.

WORDS OF OUR FAITH

The Great Commission is the command of Jesus to go, to tell, to baptize, and to share the Good News of the gospel with the people around the world.

PEOPLE

Joseph was a rich Jewish man who was a member of the Sanhedrin. He secretly believed in Jesus. He used his resources to give to Jesus a proper burial.

PLACES

Arimathea was a city about 32 kilometers northwest of Jerusalem.

THINGS

Preparation day was the day before the Sabbath and the day before the Jewish holiday.

The **Sabbath** was the day that God set aside for rest, for worship, and to help others.

To **Disciple** means to teach someone about Christ and to teach them how to follow him.

ACTIVITY

You will need these items for this activity:

- Several smooth stones, one for each child
- Markers or paint

Before class, clean all of the stones. Inspect the stones to insure that they are large enough for the children to draw or paint on them.

Say, **When Jesus arose from the dead, the stone was away from the entrance to the grave. Today, we will decorate stones to remind us of the resurrection of Jesus. Using the markers [or paints], write on your stone, "He is risen!" Then, you may decorate the stone further with the markers [or paints].**

When the children finish the decoration of their stones, let them show the stones to the class. Say, **Today we made one way to remember the resurrection of Jesus. Now we will hear about the Resurrection and about a task that Jesus gave to all of his followers.**

BIBLICAL LESSON

Prepare the following story, adapted from Matthew 27:57--28:20, before you tell it to the children.

After Jesus died, Joseph of Arimathea asked Pilate for the body of Jesus. Pilate agreed, and Joseph wrapped the body of Jesus in linen cloth. Joseph placed the body in his own tomb, and then he rolled a large stone over the entrance.

The chief priests and the Pharisees went to Pilate. They said, "Sir, Jesus said that he would rise again after three days. Give the order to guard the tomb for three days. Otherwise, his disciples will come, will steal the body, and will claim that he arose from the dead."

Pilate answered, "You may have a guard. Make the tomb as secure as possible." So they put a seal on the stone, and some soldiers guarded the tomb.

After the Sabbath, Mary Magdalene and the other Mary went to the tomb. There was a violent earthquake, and an angel descended from heaven. The angel rolled back the stone, and the angel sat upon the stone. The soldiers were terrified of the angel, and they shook and became like dead men.

The angel said to the women, "Do not be afraid. I know that you look for Jesus who died. He is not here. He arose, just as he promised that he would. See, his tomb is empty. Go and tell his disciples that Jesus arose from the dead. Also tell them that he will go ahead of them into Galilee. You will see him there."

The women hurried from the tomb. They went to tell the disciples. However, on the way, Jesus appeared to them. He greeted them, and they touched his hands and his feet. Jesus said, "Do not be afraid. Tell my disciples to meet me in Galilee. They will see me there."

The soldiers went to the city, and they reported what happened to the chief priests. The chief priests and elders devised a plan. They paid the soldiers a large sum of money. Then they said, "Tell the people that his disciples came during the night and stole the body. Then the governor will not punish you." The soldiers took the money, and they followed the plan. Many Jews still believe this story today.

The eleven disciples met Jesus in Galilee. Jesus told them, "Go and make disciples in all nations. Baptize them in the name of the Father, the Son, and the Holy Spirit. Teach them to obey everything I commanded you. I will be with you forever, even until the end of the time."

Encourage the children to answer the following questions. There are no right or wrong answers. These questions help the children to understand the story and to apply it to their lives.

1. Did the Pharisees and elders believe that Jesus would actually rise from the dead? Why did they tell the guards to lie?

2. Why did Joseph offer his own money and tomb to bury Jesus? Has someone ever sacrificed something valuable for you?

3. The passage from Matthew 28:16-20 is usually called The Great Commission. What are some ways that we can live out the command of Jesus to make disciples in all nations?

Say, **What is the best news you ever heard? The news that the disciples received on the third day after Jesus died is the best news. The disciples thought that Jesus died, and then they learned that he is alive. The resurrection of Jesus sets Christianity apart from all of the other religions. This is the good news that is still told today.**

The command that Jesus gave was to go and to make disciples throughout the entire world: to baptize them and to teach them. This command is for us as well. The objective is to reach the whole world with the message of Jesus Christ. Jesus promised that he would be with us always!

MEMORY VERSE

Practice the study's memory verse. You will find suggestions for Memory Verse Activities on pages 137-138.

ADDITIONAL ACTIVITIES

Choose from these options to enhance the children's Bible study.

1. Throughout the book of Matthew, Jesus performed many miracles. As a class, list some of the miracles. Use markers or crayons to draw illustrations of the favourite miracles of the class.

2. Research the meaning of the word "disciple." How did Jesus educate his disciples? As a class, discuss some ways that we can have the same relationship with the people in our lives.

QUESTIONS FOR BASIC COMPETITION

To prepare the children for competition, read Matthew Matthew 27:11-31 to them.

1 What did Joseph do with the body of Jesus? (27:59-60)
   1. He wrapped it in a clean linen cloth.
   2. He placed it in his own new tomb.
   3. Both answers are correct.

2 What did Joseph do at the entrance to the tomb? (27:60)
   1. He rolled a big stone in front of the tomb.
   2. He left some flowers at the tomb.
   3. He wrote the name of Jesus on the outside of the tomb.

3 How did the chief priests and the Pharisees insure that the tomb was secure? (27:66)
   1. They put a seal on the stone.
   2. They posted a guard.
   3. Both answers are correct.

4 Who went to look at the tomb at dawn on the first day of the week? (28:1)
   1. Mary Magdalene and the other Mary
   2. Peter and John
   3. Pilate

5 What happened at the tomb? (28:2)
   1. The disciples took the body of Jesus.
   2. An angel came down from heaven and rolled back the stone.
   3. A heavy rain fell.

6 What happened to the guards at the tomb of Jesus when they saw the angel? (28:4)
   1. They bowed down to the angel.
   2. They were so afraid that they shook, and they became like dead men.
   3. They became angry.

7 Who met the women as they hurried away from the tomb? (28:8-9)
   1. Jesus
   2. More angels
   3. Peter, James, and John

8 Who told to the chief priests everything that happened at the tomb? (28:11)
   1. The guards
   2. The disciples
   3. The angels

9 What did the chief priests and the elders do when the guards told them that Jesus was not in the tomb? (28:12-15)
   1. They found Jesus in the city.
   2. They planned to kill the disciples.
   3. They paid the guards to say that the disciples stole the body of Jesus.

10 What did the eleven disciples do when they went to Galilee, and they saw Jesus? (28:16-17)
   1. They ran away in fear.
   2. They worshiped him; but some of the disciples doubted.
   3. Both answers are correct.

QUESTIONS FOR ADVANCED COMPETITION

To prepare the children for competition, read Matthew 27:11-31 to them.

1 What did Joseph of Arimathea do? (27:57-58)
   1. **He asked Pilate for the body of Jesus.**
   2. He paid the chief priests because they possessed the body of Jesus.
   3. He looked for the 12 disciples.
   4. He gave a huge amount of money to the poor.

2 After the burial of Jesus, what were the Pharisees and the chief priests afraid that the disciples would do? (27:64)
   1. To raise Jesus from the dead
   2. **To steal the body of Jesus**
   3. To kill the high priest
   4. To run away and hide

3 How long would the guards make the tomb secure? (27:64)
   1. For one day
   2. Until the second day
   3. **Until the third day**
   4. For one year

4 How did the officials of Pilate make the tomb secure? (27:66)
   1. They covered the opening with dirt.
   2. They placed a lock on the door.
   3. **They placed a seal on the stone and posted a guard.**
   4. They surrounded the tomb with the chief priests and the elders.

5 Who rolled back the stone from the entrance to the tomb of Jesus? (28:2)
   1. The two women
   2. Pilate
   3. Nicodemus
   4. **An angel of the Lord**

6 What did the angel tell the women about Jesus? (28:5-7)
   1. "He has gone to be with the Father."
   2. "He is at the temple."
   3. "He is with the disciples."
   4. **"He has risen, just as he said."**

7 What did the angel tell the women to say to the disciples of Jesus? (28:7)
   1. **"He has risen from the dead and is going ahead of you into Galilee."**
   2. "It is finished. Jesus is not risen."
   3. "Go make some disciples of all nations."
   4. "Do not tell anyone about Jesus."

8 What did the chief priests give to the guards to say that the disciples of Jesus stole his body? (28:12-13)
   1. **A large sum of money**
   2. A military promotion
   3. A feast
   4. A warning

9 What did Jesus say that he possessed? (28:18)
   1. Great power
   2. **All authority in heaven and on earth**
   3. The riches of heaven
   4. Eternal life

10 In the Great Commission, what did Jesus command his disciples to do? (28:19-20)
   1. To make the disciples of all nations
   2. To baptize
   3. To teach
   4. **All of the above**

memory verses

The following verses are the memory verses for each lesson. You may reproduce this page and distribute it to the children for study purposes.

STUDY 1

"'She will give birth to a son, and you are to give him the name Jesus, because he will save his people from their sins.'" (Matthew 1:21)

STUDY 2

"Jesus answered, 'It is written: "Man does not live on bread alone, but on every word that comes from the mouth of God."'"
(Matthew 4:4)

STUDY 3

"'Blessed are the poor in spirit, for theirs is the kingdom of heaven. Blessed are those who mourn, for they will be comforted. Blessed are the meek, for they will inherit the earth. Blessed are those who hunger and thirst for righteousness, for they will be filled.'" (Matthew 5:3-6)

STUDY 4

"'Blessed are the merciful, for they will be shown mercy. Blessed are the pure in heart, for they will see God. Blessed are the peacemakers, for they will be called sons of God. Blessed are those who are persecuted because of righteousness, for theirs is the kingdom of heaven.'"(Matthew 5:7-10)

STUDY 5

"'Blessed are you when people insult you, persecute you and falsely say all kinds of evil against you because of me. Rejoice and be glad, because great is your reward in heaven, for in the same way they persecuted the prophets who were before you.'" (Matthew 5:11-12)

STUDY 6

"Your ways, O God, are holy. What god is so great as our God? You are the God who performs miracles; you display your power among the peoples." (Psalm 77:13-14)

STUDY 7

"Then he said to his disciples, 'The harvest is plentiful but the workers are few. Ask the Lord of the harvest, therefore, to send out workers into his harvest field.'" (Matthew 9:37-38)

STUDY 8

"'Come to me, all you who are weary and burdened, and I will give you rest. Take my yoke upon you and learn from me.'" (Matthew 11:28-29*a*)

STUDY 9

"'But seek first his kingdom and his righteousness, and all these things will be given to you as well.'" (Matthew 6:33)

STUDY 10

"Cast your cares on the LORD and he will sustain you; he will never let the righteous fall." (Psalm 55:22)

STUDY 11

"Simon Peter answered, 'You are the Christ, the Son of the living God.'" (Matthew 16:16)

STUDY 12

"Jesus said, 'Let the little children come to me, and do not hinder them, for the kingdom of heaven belongs to such as these.'" (Matthew 19:14)

STUDY 13

"Jesus replied: '"Love the Lord your God with all your heart and with all your soul and with all your mind." This is the first and greatest commandment. And the second is like it: "Love your neighbor as yourself."'" (Matthew 22:37-39)

STUDY 14

"'Because of the increase of wickedness, the love of most will grow cold, but he who stands firm to the end will be saved.'" (Matthew 24:12-13)

STUDY 15

"In him we have redemption through his blood, the forgiveness of sins, in accordance with the riches of God's grace." (Ephesians 1:7)

STUDY 16

"Going a little farther, he fell with his face to the ground and prayed, 'My Father, if it is possible, may this cup be taken from me. Yet not as I will, but as you will.'" (Matthew 26:39)

STUDY 17

"Then Jesus said to his disciples, 'If anyone would come after me, he must deny himself and take up his cross and follow me.'" (Matthew 16:24)

STUDY 18

"'What shall I do, then, with Jesus who is called Christ?'" (Matthew 27:22a)

STUDY 19

"'For God so loved the world that he gave his one and only Son, that whoever believes in him shall not perish but have eternal life.'" (John 3:16)

STUDY 20

"'Therefore go and make disciples of all nations, baptizing them in the name of the Father and of the Son and of the Holy Spirit, and teaching them to obey everything I have commanded you. And surely I am with you always, to the very end of the age.'" (Matthew 28:19-20)

Memory Verse Activities

Bible Pass

You will need a Bible and a source of music for this activity.

Have the children sit in a circle. Give one child the Bible. When the music starts, tell the children to pass the Bible around the circle. When the music stops, the child holding the Bible says the Bible verse. Tactfully stop the music so each child has an opportunity to say the verse.

Balloon Pop

You will need balloons, a permanent marker, and tape.

Blow up the balloons and write one word of the Bible verse on each balloon. Attach the balloons to the wall in correct order. Let the children read the verse together. Select one child to pop one balloon. Have the children recite the verse again, and remember to say the missing word. Select another child to pop a balloon. Let the children say the verse again. Continue until all the balloons are gone, and the children can recite the verse from memory.

Bible Verse Fun

Write each word or phrase of a Bible verse on a piece of paper. Make two sets, one for each team.

Divide the class into two teams. Place a set of word cards on the floor in front of each team. Scramble the order of the cards. After a signal, let the first child on each team find the first word of the verse and run to a goal line. The child places the card on the floor and races back to the second player. That child picks up the second word of the verse and races with it to the goal line. Continue until one team completes the verse in perfect order. Allow time for the second team to complete its verse. Then have both teams recite the verse together.

Bible Verse Line Up

Write each word or phrase of a Bible verse on a piece of paper.

Give each child a verse card. Instruct the children with cards to go to different parts of the room and hold up the card. Choose another child to line up the children in the correct order of the verse. Then have the class read the verse together.

Happy Faces Memory Game

Write each word or phrase of a Bible verse on a paper plate or a circular piece of paper.

Distribute the plates to the children, and ask them to draw a happy face on the blank side of the plate (circle). Attach the plates to the wall so the children can see the words of the verse. Read the verse together. Select one child to turn over one of the plates so the happy face shows. Then have the children read the verse. Select another child to turn over another plate. Say the verse again. Continue until all of the plates show happy faces, and children can recite the verse from memory.

Spider Web Review

You will need a ball of yarn.

Instruct the children to stand in a circle. Toss the ball of yarn to one child and ask him or her to say the first word of the verse. The child will wrap the yarn around his first (index) finger and toss the ball of yarn to another child across the circle. This child will say the second word of the verse and wrap the yarn around his first finger. Continue playing and saying words of the verse until every child has a turn. The back and forth motion of the yarn will produce a spider web.

Stand Up Verses

Instruct the children to sit in a circle. Instruct the first child to stand and say the first word of the verse, and then he or she sits down. The second child stands and says the second word of the verse, and then he or she sits down. Continue until the children complete the verse. Encourage the children to play again, but to go faster than the previous time. Let the children see how quickly they can say the verse.

Bible Verse Unscramble

Write each word or phrase of a Bible verse on a piece of paper.

Distribute the word cards in mixed order. Let the children arrange themselves in the correct order according to the portion of the verse they received. Have the children say the verse together. Then ask one child to turn the card around, so the other children cannot see his or her word. Have the children say the verse again. Continue in this manner until all the cards are turned around and no words are visible.

ATTENDANCE SHEET

Write the children's names in the lines provided. Place and X in the column for each lesson the child is in attendance. You may reproduce this attendance sheet if more lines are needed.

CHILD	1	2	3	4	5	6	7	8	9	10	11	12	13	14	15	16	17	18	19	20

Children's Quizzing Score Sheet

Instructions: Basic Quizzing uses only questions 1-15. Advanced Quizzing uses 20 questions. Read the Official *Rules and Procedures* for complete instructions.

Church/Team Name: _____

Names:	Round 1	1	2	3	4	5	6	7	8	9	10	11	12	13	14	15	16	17	18	19	20	Total
Team Bonus:																						Team Total

Names:	Round 2	1	2	3	4	5	6	7	8	9	10	11	12	13	14	15	16	17	18	19	20	Total
Team Bonus:																						Team Total

Names:	Round 3	1	2	3	4	5	6	7	8	9	10	11	12	13	14	15	16	17	18	19	20	Total
Team Bonus:																						Team Total

The D-Code Challenge
Bible Quizzing—Unlocked, Unlimited, and Understood

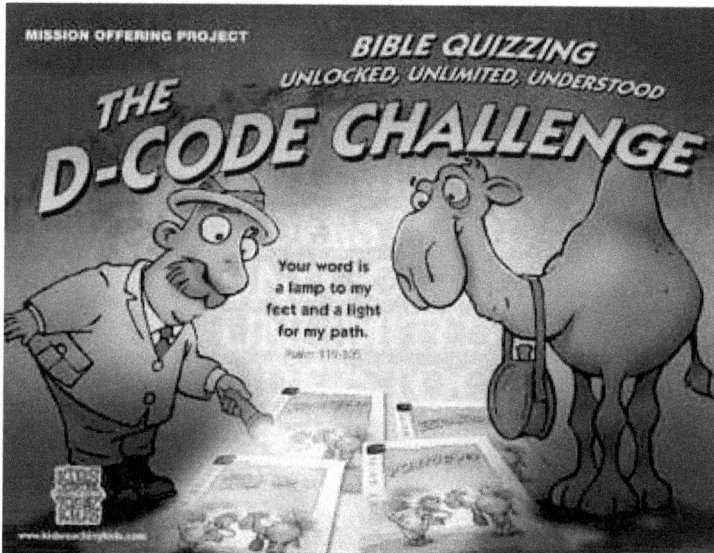

In 2008-2009, the Kids Reaching Kids Mission Offering Project, The D-Code Challenge, took on the challenge to raise funds for the translation, production, and distribution of Children's Bible Quizzing materials.

Children, districts, and churches, from all across the globe joined the effort and raised nearly $310,000 for the D-Code Challenge. The largest portion, 70% ($216,000), was designated for the Children's Bible Quizzing translation emphasis.

The book you are holding, originally produced in English by Nazarene Publishing House, was translated into Global English, French, Korean, Portuguese, and Spanish, through the efforts of individuals from   Children's Ministries International, Global Nazarene Publications, and a team of amazing translators.

Kids Reaching Kids

The Kids Reaching Kids Mission Offering Project is the annual children's mission emphasis that raises money for a number of ministry and special holistic missions efforts for children across the globe. Kids Reaching Kids encourages children, churches, districts, and world regions, to raise money to meet spiritual, educational, physical and social needs for children in every world region. For more information about Kids Reaching Kids,
visit www.kidsreachingkids.com.

www.ingramcontent.com/pod-product-compliance
Lightning Source LLC
Chambersburg PA
CBHW081541040426
42448CB00015B/3168

* 9 7 8 1 6 3 5 8 0 0 8 4 5 *